GREAT SPORTS TEAMS

THE ARIZONA DIAMONDBACKS

CHRIS HIGGINS

LUCENT BOOKS®

THOMSON
™
GALE

San Diego • Detroit • New York • San Francisco • Cleveland
New Haven, Conn. • Waterville, Maine • London • Munich

Produced by OTTN Publishing, Stockton, N.J.

© 2004 by Lucent Books. Lucent Books is an imprint of The Gale Group, Inc.,
a division of Thomson Learning, Inc.

Lucent Books® and Thomson Learning™ are trademarks used herein under license.

For more information, contact
Lucent Books
27500 Drake Rd.
Farmington Hills, MI 48331-3535
Or you can visit our Internet site at http://www.gale.com

LIBRARY OF CONGRESS CATALOGING-IN-PUBLICATION DATA

Higgins, Chris.
    The Arizona Diamondbacks / by Chris Higgins.
        p. cm. — (Great sports teams)
Includes bibliographical references and index.
Summary: Discusses the history, formation, development, and popularity of the Arizona
Diamondbacks baseball team, including a look at individual players who have had an
impact on the success of the team.
    ISBN 1-59018-303-7

Printed in the United States of America

Contents

FOREWORD

Former Supreme Court Chief Justice Warren Burger once said he always read the sports section of the newspaper first because it was about humanity's successes, while the front page listed only humanity's failures. Millions of people across the country today would probably agree with Burger's preference for tales of human endurance, record-breaking performances, and feats of athletic prowess. Although these accomplishments are far beyond what most Americans can ever hope to achieve, average people, the fans, do want to affect what happens on the field of play. Thus, their role becomes one of encouragement. They cheer for their favorite players and team and boo the opposition.

ABC Sports president Roone Arledge once attempted to explain the relationship between fan and team. Sport, said Arledge, is "a set of created circumstances—artificial circumstances—set up to frustrate a man in pursuit of a goal. He has to have certain skills to overcome those obstacles—or even to challenge them. And people who don't have those skills cheer him and admire him." Over a period of time, the admirers may develop a rabid—even irrational—allegiance to a particular team. Indeed, the word "fan" itself is derived from the word "fanatic," someone possessed by an excessive and irrational zeal. Sometimes this devotion to a team is because of a favorite player; often it's because of where a person lives, and, occasionally, it's because of a family allegiance to a particular club.

4

The Diamondbacks celebrate their World Series victory over the New York Yankees, November 4, 2001. The Arizona franchise won the championship faster than any expansion team in baseball history.

The Coming of the Diamondbacks

Phoenix was home to professional sports teams before 1998. The Phoenix Suns had been battling the premier teams in the National Basketball Association for thirty years. The Arizona Cardinals of the National Football League had relocated to the Valley of the Sun from Saint Louis in 1988; the National Hockey League's Phoenix Coyotes, formerly the Winnipeg Jets, began skating in Arizona in 1996.

But no professional sports team from Arizona had ever won a championship, and Phoenix had never hosted a major-league baseball team. As the Arizona Diamondbacks franchise prepared for its first season of play in 1998, it was clear that the citizens of Phoenix were more than ready to cheer on the new team in town. Tickets for the March 31 season opener went on sale the morning of January 10. By lunchtime, not a single ticket remained for the Diamondbacks' 50,000-seat stadium.

Most new baseball franchises have had trouble competing with established teams during their first years in the league. The Diamondbacks had no such difficulties. In only their second season, the Diamondbacks won a hundred games and finished first in their division, the National League West. In fact, Arizona captured division titles in three of its first five seasons, a truly remarkable achievement.

Most impressive, though, was what the Diamondbacks accomplished in 2001. After again winning a division title, the club disposed of its National League playoff opponents to reach the World Series. Against the heavily favored New York Yankees—the most successful franchise in the history of professional sports—the upstart Diamondbacks engineered a dramatic, come-from-behind victory in the seventh and final game. In just its fourth year of existence, the team captured baseball's biggest prize. No expansion team in baseball history has ever won a World Series faster.

With a team that includes veteran stars as well as talented newcomers, the Arizona Diamondbacks figure to add exciting new chapters to their brief but extraordinary history in the coming years. The future of the franchise appears as bright as the sun that shines, day in and day out, on the city of Phoenix.

CHAPTER 1

Winning from the Beginning

Before the late 1990s, Arizonans who wanted to go out to the ballpark to watch a professional baseball game had to content themselves with lower-level competition. Over the years, several minor-league teams played in Phoenix. And since 1947, when the Cleveland Indians and New York Giants first came to Arizona for spring training, major-league clubs have played in the Cactus League. But aside from helping ballplayers get back into shape and helping managers and coaches determine who will be on their regular-season rosters, spring-training games are essentially meaningless. The big-leaguers always left before the 100-degree summer heat descended on Arizona. Thus, as fans in other areas of the country flocked to stadiums to cheer their hometown heroes on to a pennant, Arizonans could only follow their favorite players and teams by reading newspapers, listening to the radio, or watching television.

Man with a Plan

For Arizonans who longed to root for a home team, March 9, 1995, marked an important milestone. On that day a group of investors led by Jerry Colangelo, the owner of the Phoenix

Baseball commissioner Bud Selig (left) and Arizona businessman Jerry Colangelo leave a meeting. A group of investors headed by Colangelo was granted the Diamondbacks franchise in March 1995.

Suns, was awarded the franchise for a new major-league baseball team. The team, which would be based in Phoenix and compete in the National League West Division, was slated to debut in 1998. (Another new franchise, the Tampa Bay Devil Rays, was scheduled to join the American League at the same time.) Colangelo and his partners paid major-league baseball more than $130 million for the new ball club, the Arizona Diamondbacks.

For Jerry Colangelo, the Diamondbacks represented the culmination of a longtime dream. In 1991 he and a group of fellow investors had made a serious bid to attract a major-league expansion team to Phoenix. Their hopes were dashed when Denver was awarded the franchise instead. Since that time, Colangelo and his partners had watched with envy as the Colorado Rockies built spectacular Coors Field and filled the stadium with millions of fans each year. When the next baseball franchises became available, the Phoenix group vowed not to be shut out again.

After Colangelo's group of investors was granted the Diamondbacks franchise, the next step was to provide a place for the team to play. Government leaders in Maricopa County, where Phoenix is located, contributed to the cause by approving a tax increase to help pay for construction of a new stadium.

In addition to comfortable seating for fans and a high-quality field of natural grass, modern major-league ballparks include a host of amenities, including corporate luxury suites, concession stands and restaurants, spacious offices for the team's management, and a plush clubhouse, well-appointed locker rooms, and state-of-the-art exercise rooms for the players. Given the stifling heat of Arizona summers, the Diamondbacks' stadium would also require a retractable roof and air conditioning. Ground was broken for the stadium on November 16, 1995.

Visionary Philosophy

From the beginning, the Diamondbacks announced that they intended to be different from previous expansion franchises. The team adopted a mission statement that read, "The Arizona Diamondbacks' mission is to establish a winning tradition that embodies the genuine spirit of baseball; an organization to which all Arizonans will point with pride, which conducts its business with integrity and community responsibility; so that Arizona's children will grow up knowing the rich tradition that has made baseball America's national pastime."[1]

In this spirit the owners hired Buck Showalter as manager in November 1995. Showalter was a no-nonsense baseball man and leader; as skipper of the New York Yankees he had been named American League Manager of the Year in 1994 and had led the Yankees to a wild-card playoff spot in 1995. Showalter was also a family man who liked nothing better than to relax at home with his collection of videotaped episodes of *The Andy Griffith Show*. He was just the kind of person Arizona's owners wanted to represent the new team.

Baseball veteran Buck Showalter was hired as Arizona's first manager.

Because the team was starting from scratch, a farm system for training minor-league prospects had to be created. A Diamondbacks training facility was opened in the Dominican Republic. The Lethbridge Mounties of Alberta, Canada, became a Diamondbacks farm team and were renamed the Lethbridge Black Diamonds. Other prospects played for minor-league teams in the Arizona League. Scouts fanned out across the world, signing players wherever they found them—even as far away as Australia.

The team set high standards, doing what it took to become a top-notch baseball organization. Even the most marginal prospects were given the best equipment, time to learn, and respect. Pinstriped uniforms were designed in the team's colors—purple, turquoise, copper, and white. The spirit of being different even influenced the unique design of Bank One Ballpark—the only major league baseball stadium that features a swimming pool in the outfield.

As their 1998 debut approached, the Diamondbacks began filling their roster with the best ballplayers they could find. Veteran shortstop Jay Bell was signed, along with slugging third baseman Matt Williams; they joined promising young infielders Tony Batista and Travis Lee. The team picked up experienced pitchers like Andy Benes, Willie Blair, Greg Olsen, Chuck McElroy, and Omar Daal. Other additions included catcher Jorge Fabregas and outfielders Karim Garcia and Devon White. The players were pleased to be in Arizona. Williams, a star with the Cleveland Indians, had given up millions of dollars to get out of his contract with Cleveland so he could play in Phoenix, where his family lived.

Play Ball!

On March 31, 1998, the grass was thick and green under the retractable roof of Bank One Ballpark. A sellout crowd of 50,179 fans packed the stands as Andy Benes took the mound to deliver the first pitch in Diamondbacks' history. Though the Colorado Rockies tagged Benes for five runs and the Diamondbacks lost, Arizona fans in attendance could say they saw a lot of firsts. Travis Lee wrote his name large in Diamondbacks' history that Tuesday night: Lee collected the club's first hit (a first-inning single), its first homer, its first run batted in (RBI), and its first run scored.

Diamondbacks pitcher Andy Benes delivers the first pitch in the team's first game, March 31, 1998.

For an expansion team in its first season, low expectations are the rule. Besting the established organizations is very difficult. In 1998 the Diamondbacks were no exception: they finished fifth in the National League West with a record of sixty-five wins and ninety-seven losses. (The expansion Devil Rays, also playing their first season in 1998, posted a similar record: 63-99.)

Some franchises, such as the Chicago Cubs and the Colorado Rockies, attract good crowds year after year, even when the team is not very good. This was not the case in Arizona, however. After the disappointing first season, the Diamondbacks' season-ticket sales dropped. The owners decided that the best way to keep people coming to the ballpark was to put a winning team on the field. Joe Garagiola Jr., a team executive, later noted, "At that time Jerry [Colangelo] said, 'Look, it appears to me that we are not going to be beneficiaries of an extended honeymoon period as has been the case in other cities. So it looks like in order for us to protect the enormous investment that has now been made in this franchise, we are going to have to see what we can do to become competitive sooner, rather than later.'"[2] This meant signing big-name free-agent players.

A Taste of Success

Over the winter of 1998–1999, the Diamondbacks made headlines with the signing of star pitchers Randy Johnson and Todd Stottlemyre. They also signed lesser-known players like Luis Gonzalez, Tony Womack, and a rookie pitcher from Korea named Byung-Hyun Kim. These moves paid off in a big way. The 1999 Arizona team pulled off one of the biggest turnarounds in baseball history, winning its division with a 100-62 record. The club reached the playoffs in only its second season of existence, a major-league baseball record.

Although Arizona lost the National League Division Series to the New York Mets, three games to one, the team had many reasons to be proud. Members of the Diamondbacks had compiled some impressive statistics. Johnson posted a 17-9 record, with 364 strikeouts and a 2.48 earned run average (ERA)—stats that helped him win the 1999 National League Cy Young Award as the league's top pitcher. Another Arizona pitcher, Omar Daal, won sixteen games in 1999. Jay Bell led the team with thirty-eight home runs, while Matt Williams hit thirty-five and Steve Finley thirty-four. Outfielder Luis Gonzalez chipped in with a career-best twenty-six homers and finished with a .336 batting average. The team had turned a corner, and there was plenty of talent to build on for the future.

After the successful 1999 season, Arizona took a step backward in 2000. Though they remained in contention for most of the year, the Diamondbacks managed to win just twelve of thirty games in September and finished third in the division with an 85-77 record.

After the season, Showalter was fired. Team management felt the skipper's strictness had been part of the reason the club had faltered down the stretch. "We think it's time to move in another direction," Colangelo told reporters. "We think it's time to work on a new attitude in the organization, in the clubhouse. . . . Buck Showalter is an intense guy in everything he does. . . . But you also need to have an atmosphere that's conducive for players to perform at the best of their ability."[3]

There were some bright spots during the 2000 season. Johnson won another Cy Young Award, and late in the season Arizona traded for another top-line starting pitcher, Curt Schilling. Together, Johnson and Schilling would give the team a powerful one-two combination on the mound.

A New Skipper at the Helm

Bob Brenly received the nod as the team's new manager before the 2001 season. Brenly, who had been working as an announcer for the Diamondbacks, was a former major-leaguer; his playing career had lasted from 1981 to 1989. Although he had some previous coaching experience, 2001 would be his first season as a manager. However, he had been around the Diamondbacks for a few years, and he confessed to reporters that he liked the team's chances. "Perhaps I'm a ridiculous optimist," Brenly said, "but I really [do] feel this team [is] ready to win."[4]

From his first day on the job, the new manager lightened things up. "Those are the old rules," he said as he dropped a copy of Showalter's rulebook in the wastebasket. He read his three new rules to the team: "One, curfew of 1 A.M. . . . Two, be on time. Three, get it done."[5]

The team responded immediately to Brenly's more relaxed style. Arizona opened the season with a 3-2 win for the new manager. "From day one when he threw down the rules, we all knew we were in this together," said Luis Gonzalez. "We've all moved around and have had tough journeys. We see the mountain, now. Now, we want to get to the top."[6]

Arizona's stars led the way as the team fought for the lead in the National League West. Luis Gonzalez won National League Player of the Month honors in April after knocking thirteen home runs. Curt Schilling went 5-1 in May and was named NL Pitcher of the Month. In June, Gonzalez hit a scorching .417 and was again selected as Player of the Month.

On August 11 the Diamondbacks took the division lead for good. Schilling and Johnson were clearly the two best pitchers in the league, and on September 5, Schilling notched his twentieth victory to become the first twenty-game winner in the franchise's brief history.

There was magic happening in the Valley of the Sun. But suddenly events that unfolded at the other end of the country made the pennant chase in Phoenix seem insignificant.

Baseball in a Time of Loss

On the morning of September 11, 2001, terrorists hijacked four passenger planes shortly after takeoff from East Coast airports. The terrorists crashed one into each tower of New York City's World Trade Center and one into the Pentagon near Washington, D.C. The fourth jetliner went down in a field in western Pennsylvania after a struggle between passengers and the hijackers. More than 3,000 people lost their lives in the attacks.

The tragedy shocked the nation, and people everywhere paused for a period of mourning and reflection. Out of respect, the commissioner of baseball postponed all games, and no one was sure whether the 2001 season would resume.

A week after the attacks, baseball officials decided to finish the season. Americans started to tune in to baseball again, and the game provided a welcome relief from the stress and sadness of the time.

"In a strange way, and maybe it's God's timing on the whole thing, baseball served a very unique role in this country as we came out of 9/11," observed Jerry Colangelo. "There was this great emphasis on our country, our spirituality and the American flag. People once again were kind to one another. It just changed so much and baseball was part of the tonic of bringing people back."[7]

The time off did not slow down the Diamondbacks, as the team kept winning. Arizona was in a tight race with the San Francisco Giants for the division title. On October 5, the Diamondbacks won their ninety-second game of the season with a 5-0 shutout of the Milwaukee Brewers. Although Arizona lost its final two games of the season, the team finished with a 92-70 record and a two-game lead over the Giants. For the second time in three years, the Diamondbacks were division champions.

It had been a team effort. Gonzalez had turned in a monster season, hitting .325 with fifty-seven home runs and 142 RBIs. Outfielder Reggie Sanders walloped thirty-three homers and drove in ninety runs. Infielder Craig Counsell hit .275 and scored seventy-six

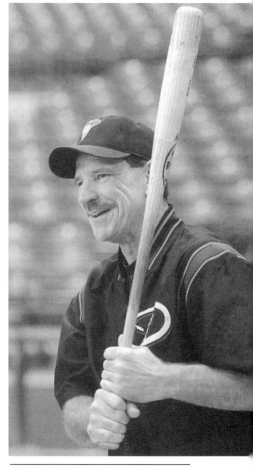

After the disappointing 2000 season, the Diamondbacks hired Bob Brenly as manager. The team flourished in 2001 under his less-restrictive management style.

runs, while Mark Grace hit .298 with fifteen home runs and seventy-eight RBIs. Johnson and Schilling both won more than twenty games, and the teammates finished first and second in the voting for the Cy Young Award.

While people across the nation supported New York after the World Trade Center tragedy, in Arizona that did not mean rooting for the Yankees.

A Magical Run

In the first round of the playoffs, Arizona faced the St. Louis Cardinals. The Diamondbacks triumphed in five games, thanks to masterful pitching by Schilling and clutch hitting by Tony Womack, to advance to the National League Championship Series, where they would face the powerhouse Atlanta Braves. This time solid pitching from Johnson, Schilling, and Kim helped the Diamondbacks win their first National League pennant. The Diamondbacks now moved on to the biggest series in baseball.

Many great teams and players never get a chance to even compete in the World Series. The Diamondbacks' roster included twenty-one players who had never appeared in the Fall Classic. Pitcher Mike Morgan was one of them, and he had toiled for more than twenty years in the majors.

All of Arizona was abuzz with talk of a championship, but victory would not be easy. The Diamondbacks would be facing the most successful baseball franchise of all time, the New York Yankees. The Yankees had won the World Series in four of the previous five seasons, including the last three in a row. They were heavy favorites. The Yankees featured excellent hitters such as Bernie Williams, Derek Jeter, David Justice, and Tino Martinez, and strong pitchers like Roger Clemens and Andy Pettitte. For many people, the Yankees were also sentimental favorites because of the horrors that New York had experienced on September 11 and the courageous way that New Yorkers had responded to the tragedy.

Despite their underdog status, the Diamondbacks won the first two games at Bank One Ballpark, showing that they would not be intimidated. But then the series moved to Yankee Stadium, which is steeped in baseball lore and alive with the Yankee mystique. It is one of the most difficult places for an opposing team to play, as Randy Johnson noted. Johnson, who earlier in his career had pitched in playoff games against the Yankees, had important advice for his teammates. "There's a lot of guys on this team, like Mark Grace, who have never been to Yankee Stadium," he said. "It's going to be the ride of your life. So when we get there, I can tell them this: 'Buckle up!'"[8]

Johnson's prediction about the difficulty of playing at storied Yankee Stadium came true, however, as Arizona lost three tough games in a row. New York won game three behind the nearly unhittable pitching of Roger Clemens and Mariano Rivera. Then the Yankees put together a pair of dramatic, late-inning rallies to pull out games four and five. "This is the most incredible couple of games I've ever managed,"[9] said

Yankee skipper Joe Torre after the thrilling come-from-behind victories.

Though the extra-inning losses were hard to swallow, the Diamondbacks did not dwell on them. The series returned to Arizona for game six, in which the Diamondbacks exploded for fifteen runs to win in a laugher. In the decisive seventh game, New York was leading 2-1 in the bottom of the ninth inning, with the dominating Rivera on the mound. But Arizona took a page from New York's book, rallying to tie the game before Gonzalez hit a bloop single to score Jay Bell with the winning run. Arizona players mobbed them at home plate: The Diamondbacks were world champions. "I didn't have to hit it hard—just loop something out there and get it in play," said an excited Gonzalez. "This is a dream come true."[10]

The Diamondbacks had won their first World Series. It was also the first championship for any major-league sports team in Arizona. "They certainly earned it,"[11] admitted a disappointed Torre. Even New York's staunchest supporters were impressed by the Diamondbacks and gracious in defeat. "That was the greatest Game 7 ever," commented the mayor of New York City, Rudy Giuliani, although he admitted that "as a Yankees fan I wish it had turned out differently."[12]

A Competitive Team

The Diamondbacks came back in 2002 ready to defend their championship. They finished first in the National League West again with a 98-64 record, and once again Johnson, Schilling, Kim, and Gonzalez turned in impressive regular-season performances. Johnson and Schilling each won more than twenty games and struck out more than three hundred batters, and Byung-Hyun Kim notched thirty-six saves. Gonzalez pounded twenty-eight home runs and drove in 103 runs. However, the star outfielder separated his shoulder during the final days of the season, and without Gonzalez's powerful bat in the lineup the Diamondbacks fell to St. Louis in the first round of the playoffs.

Arizona faced many challenges during the 2003 season. Schilling and Johnson were both hurt early, and they struggled to get back into the lineup. Matt Williams retired in June, and Kim was traded to the Boston Red Sox.

Arizona's Junior Spivey slides home safe during a September 2003 game against San Francisco.

But there were many bright spots as well. Rookie starting pitcher Brandon Webb averaged nearly one strikeout per inning and was among the top vote-getters for the National League's Rookie of the Year. Alex Cintron emerged as the team's shortstop, batting over .300 in his first season of full-time play. They helped the Diamondbacks remain in the race for the National League's wild-card playoff spot until the last weeks of the season.

Missing the 2003 playoffs was certainly a disappointment for the Diamondbacks and their fans. But the mix of star veterans and talented youngsters on the Arizona roster makes it a safe bet that the franchise will be a force in the National League for years to come.

CHAPTER 2

Randy Johnson

Randy Johnson's fastball has been clocked at more than one hundred miles an hour, but the left-hander does much more than just throw hard. Johnson pitches with control and variety, and he can just as easily strike out a batter with a change-up as with a fastball. At six-foot-ten, "the Big Unit" is the tallest person ever to play in the major leagues. Since the mid-1990s, Johnson has been one of the best pitchers in baseball. He won five Cy Young Awards, including four straight from 1999 to 2002.

Humble Beginnings

Randall David Johnson was born in Walnut Creek, California, on September 10, 1963. He was the youngest of six children born to Carol and Rollen Johnson. When Randy was young, the family moved south to Livermore, which is about forty miles southeast of San Francisco.

Height ran in the family. Rollen "Bud" Johnson, who worked as a policeman, stood six-foot-six. When Randy entered grade school, he was one of the tallest children in his class, and his height attracted attention. "I was the object of everyone's jokes and teases, and it hurt,"[13] he later recalled. Randy compensated for his feelings of self-consciousness by becoming a class clown. His parents were sympathetic, but they were also strict; they made sure his classroom antics did not get in the way of his schoolwork.

Randy began playing Little League baseball as soon as he was old enough. His height gave him an advantage on the field: He found that he could throw the ball much faster than his peers. But he was also wild, and to improve his control he began throwing pitches against the family garage. Bud Johnson noticed that the pitches were slowly demolishing the wooden garage, but he encouraged his son to keep practicing.

Randy entered Livermore High School in 1978, and he made the varsity baseball team as a sophomore. Livermore coach Eric Hoff taught the lanky hurler to throw an assortment of pitches instead of relying on his ninety-mile-per-hour fastball. This made him even more effective, and he struck out opposing batters by the dozens. Randy saved his most spectacular high school performance for his last game: He pitched a perfect game, notching thirteen strikeouts, before a stadium filled with spectators and major-league scouts.

College Baseball

The Atlanta Braves were one of the teams that took note of the teenaged hurler. Atlanta selected Johnson in the third round of the 1982 free-agent draft and offered him $60,000 to sign a contract. But several colleges were offering him scholarships. It was a difficult choice. On the one hand, $60,000 was a lot of money for a nineteen-year-old to turn down, and if he went to college and sustained a serious injury, he might never get the chance to play pro ball. On the other hand, signing with Atlanta now was no guarantee that he would ever make it out of the minor leagues. It was entirely possible that he might blow his arm out pitching for one of the Braves' farm teams, and then what would he do?

His parents and coach urged him to go to college, and in the end Johnson took their advice. A college diploma would at least give him a way to make a living if his professional baseball career did not work out. "I'd seen too many of my friends sign and then get hurt,"[14] he said.

Johnson pitches in a game for the University of Southern California, which he attended from 1982 to 1985. His decision to go to college rather than sign a professional baseball contract right after high school was a difficult one.

Johnson accepted a full scholarship to the University of Southern California. The scholarship was originally to play both baseball and basketball, but in his sophomore season Johnson decided to concentrate on baseball. USC's baseball team, coached by Rod Dedeaux, was one of the best in the country. One of Johnson's teammates was slugger Mark McGwire, who would eventually hit 583 home runs in the major leagues. At USC Johnson had to work hard both in the classroom and on the baseball field to keep his scholarship.

As a member of the Trojans' baseball team Johnson earned a reputation as a flake. In the middle of games he would talk to the ball and curse his mistakes when the pressure got to him. Johnson also experienced problems with wildness; at times he was unable to throw the ball over the plate. Though he sometimes grew frustrated by his inconsistent performance, experts continued to believe in his talent. *Baseball America* rated Johnson the fourth-best pitching prospect in 1985. That year, he was drafted by the Montreal Expos. Johnson signed a contract with the Expos and began playing professional ball in the minor leagues.

To the Majors

Randy Johnson worked his way up to the major leagues quickly. He spent less than three full seasons in the minors before being called up by the Expos at the tail end of the 1988 season. He appeared in his first major-league game on September 15, 1988, against the Pittsburgh Pirates. Johnson gave up two home runs and walked six batters in five innings, but was credited with the victory. He finished the season with a respectable 3-0 record, twenty-five strikeouts, seven walks, and a 2.42 earned run average.

Johnson started the 1989 season as the number-two pitcher in the Expos' pitching rotation, but after an 0-4 start he was sent back to the club's Class-AAA minor-league affiliate in Indianapolis. Johnson worked on his mechanics in three games with Indianapolis, but he would not return to the Expos. Instead, he was traded to the Seattle Mariners for veteran pitcher Mark Langston.

Johnson pitched his first game for Seattle against the New York Yankees on May 30, 1989. He opened the game by striking out perhaps the best leadoff hitter in baseball history, Ricky Henderson, and went on to get the victory. The rest of his season, however, was not quite as successful. He finished with a mediocre 7-9 record and a 4.40 ERA.

Over the winter Johnson lifted weights and practiced under the eye of Mariners pitching coach Mike Paul. The off-season work paid dividends during the 1990 season. On June 2, 1990, Johnson threw the first no-hitter in Mariners history, beating the Detroit Tigers, 2-0. He was named to the American League All-Star team that year, and he finished the season with a 14-11 record. His control was still not good, however, as he led the league with 120 walks.

Gaining Control

Though he led the league in walks in the next two seasons, Johnson started to gain control over his pitches in 1992—with some help from Nolan Ryan. Like Johnson, the strikeout king and future Hall of Famer featured a blazing fastball but sometimes struggled with wildness. When the two worked together on a training video during 1992, Ryan showed Johnson how changing his pitching motion would give him better control. As Johnson adjusted his delivery, he found that he could throw harder with greater accuracy. Ryan found out just how much Johnson had learned when the two faced each other in a game during the summer of 1992. In that contest the Big Unit struck out eighteen batters. Over the course of the season, Johnson collected 241 strikeouts, leading the American League. It was the first of four consecutive strikeout titles he would win. From 1992 to 1995, Johnson would strike out more than a thousand batters.

Johnson married his girlfriend Lisa after the 1992 season and signed a one-year contract with the Mariners for $2.625 million. Everything seemed to be going his way, but in December his father died. Johnson was heartbroken and depressed, and he considered leaving baseball. However, he decided that his father would have wanted him to continue.

When Johnson reported to spring training for the 1993 season, the Mariners had a new manager, Lou Pinella. Seattle's owners and fans hoped that the fiery Pinella could reverse the Mariners' losing ways, which were of long standing. In fact, since entering the American League as an expansion team in 1977, Seattle had enjoyed only one winning record—an 83-79 mark during the 1991 season. Under Pinella, the Mariners eked

From 1993 to 1997, Johnson was the most dominant pitcher in the American League, winning 80 percent of his decisions.

out a second winning season, finishing the 1993 campaign at 82-80. But Johnson emerged as one of the league's best pitchers, posting a 19-8 record and winning a spot in the All-Star Game for the second time.

The following season, 1994, was shortened by a players' strike. Before the suspension of play, Johnson hammered out a 13-6 record for another lackluster Mariners team, which finished 49-63. Frustrated by the team's struggles, Johnson asked to be traded. "I'm one of the best pitchers playing for one of the worst teams in baseball,"[15] he complained.

Outside of his baseball disappointments, however, life was pretty good for Johnson. In December he and his wife, Lisa, welcomed their first child, a daughter they named Samantha.

Ups and Downs

Johnson became less frustrated professionally in 1995 as the Mariners put together their best season ever. A strong September surge enabled them to finish the shortened season with a 79-66 record, tied with the Anaheim Angels atop the American League West. Offensively, stars like Ken Griffey Jr. and Edgar Martinez powered the team. Johnson was the Mariners' best pitcher. He posted an amazing 18-2 record with 294 strikeouts and a 2.48 ERA, statistics that won him the American League's Cy Young Award. Johnson's most important victory of 1995 came in a playoff for the AL West title against Anaheim. He threw a masterful three-hitter to beat the Angels and clinch the division title, putting Seattle in the playoffs for the first time.

In the best-of-five division series, the Mariners faced the New York Yankees, who had reached the playoffs as the wild-card team. The Yankees came out strong by winning the first two games. Johnson stopped them in game three, giving up just two runs, and Seattle evened the series by winning the next game. In game five the Yankees had an early lead, but Seattle managed to tie the game. When Seattle reliever Norm Charlton gave up two hits in the top of the ninth inning, Pinella sent Johnson into the game in relief. He got out of the inning by striking out Wade Boggs and inducing two pop-ups. After the Yankees shut down Seattle in the bottom of the ninth, the game went into extra innings. Johnson notched three more strikeouts in the tenth, but Seattle failed to score in its half of the inning. In the top of the eleventh inning, an exhausted Johnson gave up a run. He battled back and ended the inning by striking out Jim Leyritz and Paul O'Neill. In the bottom of the eleventh Seattle scored two runs to win the game and the playoff series.

Seattle moved on to face the Cleveland Indians in the American League Championship Series. Mariners fans had high hopes, but the Indians proved to be the better team. Johnson won game three for Seattle, but he was out of gas for game six of the series. He pitched with heart but left with his team down 4-0. Cleveland went on to the World Series, while the Mariners went home.

In April 1996, the Johnsons celebrated the birth of their second child, son Tanner. However, there was little for Johnson to celebrate on the field. He missed most of the 1996 season with a back injury and required extensive rehabilitation before he would be able to pitch again. The work paid off in 1997, though, as he finished the season with an excellent 20-4 record, 291 strikeouts, and a 2.28 ERA. The Mariners finished 90-72 to win the American League West again, but Johnson pitched poorly in the playoffs. He lost two games to Baltimore, and the Orioles knocked Seattle out of the postseason.

Johnson dominated the American League between 1994 and 1997. In eighty-one starts during that period, he won fifty-three games and lost just nine. Randy Johnson had clearly become one of baseball's best pitchers. It was obvious that he could command a huge salary on the free-agent market when he became eligible at the end of the 1998 season. The Mariners were afraid they would lose their ace pitcher as a free agent without getting anything in return, so they began considering trade offers before the start of the season.

Johnson started 1998 with Seattle, but he pitched poorly as trade rumors swirled. In July he was dealt to the Houston Astros, a National League team that was making a playoff run. Johnson finished strong for the Astros, going 10-1 with a 1.28 ERA for Houston. The Big Unit proved that he could overpower National League hitters as easily as he had overpowered batters in the American League. He struck out ten or more players in seventeen different games during the 1998 season. In

Autograph-seeking fans thrust baseballs at Johnson as he takes a break during spring training in 1998. With a year until he could become a free agent, trade rumors swirled around the pitcher.

the playoffs, however, he again faltered. Although he did not pitch badly in the 1998 division series, Houston lost both games in which he appeared.

Diamondback Days

When Randy Johnson became a free agent at the end of the 1998 season, Jerry Colangelo was the first person to contact him. The Diamondbacks owner met with Johnson and told him that the new franchise was committed to winning. Johnson agreed to a four-year contract worth more than $52 million. "I believe 110 percent I've made the right decision," he said. "I feel I can win here."[16]

Johnson was correct. In his second start of the 1999 season, on April 10, he set a team record by striking out fifteen batters.

He continued to fan hitters at a phenomenal pace. On August 26, he struck out his three-hundredth batter of the season, reaching that mark faster than any other pitcher in history. He also became the first hurler to strike out more than three hundred batters in both the American and National Leagues. Johnson finished the year with 364 strikeouts, by far the best figure in the National League. He also led the league in complete games and in innings pitched. He finished with a 17-9 record and a 2.48 earned run average, good enough to garner his second Cy Young Award. He was just the third pitcher to win the award in both the American and National Leagues.

Arizona was a vastly improved team in 1999, thanks to Johnson and the team's other stars. The Diamondbacks finished with a record of 100-62, winning thirty-five games more than they had in the previous season. The commitment to winning that Colangelo had promised seemed to be paying off.

In the first round of the playoffs, Johnson started the opening game against the New York Mets. The Mets took an early 4-1 lead, but Arizona rallied to tie the game in the bottom of the sixth inning. Johnson pitched into the ninth inning, but loaded the bases before being pulled with one out. Reliever Bobby Chouinard got a second out, but New York's Edgardo Alfonzo then pounded a grand-slam home run to give the Mets an 8-4 win. Johnson, charged with seven of the runs, took the loss. It was his sixth straight postseason defeat, which set a major-league record.

"It's obviously not the way I would've [written] the script," a disappointed Johnson said after the game. "Hopefully, I'll have another chance to pitch against those guys."[17] Johnson would not have another opportunity to break his losing streak in 1999, though, as the Diamondbacks fell to the Mets in four games.

In 2000 Johnson had another superb year. He notched his three-thousandth career strikeout on September 10, 2000, and finished with a 19-7 record, 347 strikeouts, and a 2.64 ERA. For the third time, he received the Cy Young Award as the league's best pitcher. However, the 2000 Diamondbacks finished with a disappointing 85-77 record and did not reach the playoffs.

One of the most important moments of the season occurred when the team traded for pitcher Curt Schilling in midseason.

Schilling's arrival helped Johnson in many ways, as they became friends. They also learned from each other. Having another top-line starter on the staff took some of the pressure off the Big Unit. A more-relaxed Johnson surprised his teammates by joking and goofing around in the clubhouse, although he maintained his intensity when on the mound. "I'm supposed to be mean and nasty," Johnson cautioned reporters who asked about his relaxed attitude. "Don't let the word get out."[18]

Road to the World Series

In 2001 the Diamondbacks started winning under new manager Bob Brenly. One of Johnson's best games came against the Cincinnati Reds on May 8, 2001, when he struck out twenty batters over nine innings. He did not get credit for the victory, because he left the game with the score tied, but Arizona eventually won in eleven innings. And even though the strikeout total tied a major-league record shared by Roger Clemens and Kerry Wood, Johnson did not get his name in the record books because the game had gone into extra innings. This was the third time in his major-league career that Johnson had struck out nineteen or more batters.

Throughout the 2001 season, Johnson and Schilling proved they were the two best pitchers in the National League. Sportswriters and fans began to compare them with such potent pitching combinations as Sandy Koufax and Don Drysdale, who had starred for the Dodgers during the 1960s. Johnson and Schilling would finish the season with a combined 665 strikeouts and forty-three victories—almost half of the team's wins that year.

When Arizona won the division, Johnson was ready to end his playoff losing streak. "I feel as if the responsibility of carrying the team in the postseason has been evenly divided,"[19] he commented. His struggles were not over, however. After Schilling pitched a gem to win the first game of the series against St. Louis, Johnson dropped the second game, 4-1. Arizona ultimately prevailed, winning the series in five games thanks to another fine performance by Schilling in the final contest.

In Arizona, Johnson teamed up with Curt Schilling to provide an
unstoppable one-two pitching punch during the 2001 season.

The National League Championship Series would match
Arizona against the Atlanta Braves, a team that had dominated
the league for nearly a decade. The Braves were perhaps the
only team with a pitching staff as talented as Arizona's, led by
ace starters Greg Maddux and Tom Glavine. In the first game
of the series, Johnson would face Maddux, a crafty veteran
who had won four National League Cy Young Awards.

Johnson broke his seven-game playoff losing streak with
a dominating performance. After giving up a first-inning single
to Chipper Jones, he retired twenty straight Atlanta batters.
He finished with a complete-game three-hit shutout, striking
out eleven batters and walking just one. "He was flat-out

awesome," Atlanta's Jones said after the game. "Truly the best I've ever seen him."[20]

Johnson would win again in game five of the series, outdueling Glavine, 3-2. Arizona was headed to the World Series for the first time.

Winning It All

Although baseball experts were impressed by the Diamondbacks' resilience, it seemed unlikely they could beat the Yankees. But Arizona took the first game, then Johnson hurled a three-hit, complete-game shutout in game two to give his team the series lead. He was practically unhittable. "He's certainly the same nightmare that I remember him being in Seattle,"[21] commented New York's Chuck Knoblauch. Infielder Luis Sojo agreed. "He was amazing," said Sojo. "He had every pitch working."[22] A three-run homer from Matt Williams made the game fun for Johnson. "I felt like I could go out and enjoy it,"[23] he said.

The next three games proved anything but enjoyable for the Diamondbacks, as the Yankees won all three to take the series lead. It was up to Johnson to stop New York in game six. The Big Unit got a lot of help from his teammates: The Diamondbacks pounded twenty-two hits and scored fifteen runs

Johnson delivers a pitch to New York's Bernie Williams during game two of the 2001 World Series. The Arizona ace allowed just three hits in the game and shut out the Yankees.

to rout the Yankees. Johnson left the game after seven innings, leaving open the possibility that he might be able to pitch in relief if needed in the seventh game of the series.

Schilling started the seventh game and again pitched well, but he tired with one out in the eighth, allowing a home run that gave New York a 2-1 lead. Johnson was brought into the game to relieve his friend. He finished the eighth and ninth innings without giving up a run. And, when Arizona rallied for two runs to win the game in the bottom of the ninth, Johnson and his teammates ran out of the dugout howling with delight—they were world champions!

Johnson had finally won a World Series title, and he did it in style. He was one of just a handful of pitchers to win three games during a World Series. He and Schilling were named co-MVPs of the series. A few weeks later Johnson received the 2001 Cy Young Award for his 21-6 record, 2.49 earned run average, and league-best 372 strikeouts.

Good Things Will Accumulate

In 2002 Johnson won his fourth-straight Cy Young Award with a 24-5 record, 334 strikeouts, and a 2.32 ERA. The Diamondbacks again finished first in their division, but they were not destined for another trip to the World Series. Arizona lost three games in a row to St. Louis in the division series. Johnson pitched well in the opener, giving up just two runs, but he nevertheless lost the game.

In 2003 Johnson signed a two-year, $33 million contract extension with Arizona that will keep him in Phoenix through 2005. He was characteristically low-key about the deal: "I just want to go about my business, work hard and know that if I go out there every fifth day and prepare the way I have been, that good things will happen on the fifth day and after the course of the season good things will accumulate."[24]

Good things have accumulated for Randy Johnson, both in his career and in his personal life. In addition to their older children Samantha and Tanner, Lisa and Randy Johnson have two other daughters, Willow (born in April 1998) and Alexandria (born in December 1999). Throughout his career Johnson has been active in a number of charities. He has donated tens of

Randy Johnson tips his hat to acknowledge an ovation, August 10, 2002. Johnson had just recorded his 3,641st strikeout, moving him past Tom Seaver into fifth place on baseball's all-time strikeout list.

thousands of dollars to organizations that help homeless people, and in 1999 he received an award for his charity work to combat cystic fibrosis.

A knee injury early in 2003 made the season a disappointing one personally for Randy Johnson, but as his playing days near an end he has established himself as perhaps the most dominating pitcher of his generation. By the end of the 2003 season he was ranked fourth on the list for career strikeouts. He has won more than 230 games in his career, and only one other pitcher, Roger Clemens, has won more than Johnson's five Cy Young Awards. It is clear that when Randy Johnson does decide to hang up his spikes, he is a strong candidate for induction into the Baseball Hall of Fame.

CHAPTER 3

Curt Schilling

When Curt Schilling joined Randy Johnson in Arizona, he became part of one of the best pitching combinations in baseball history. Schilling's success comes from hard work, talent, and determination, as well as a willingness to learn from others. He has improved with age—in his first two seasons with the Diamondbacks, he won twenty-two and twenty-three games and twice was runner-up for the Cy Young Award.

Born to Pitch

Curtis Montague Schilling was born on November 14, 1966, in Anchorage, Alaska. His father, Cliff, was a soldier in the U.S. Army, so the Schilling family moved around quite a bit as Cliff was transferred from post to post. The Schillings settled in Phoenix, Arizona, about the time Curt entered kindergarten.

Cliff Schilling passed down his love of sports to Curt, specifically a love for the Pittsburgh Pirates and Steelers. On September 30, 1972, Cliff took his son to see his first professional baseball game. For Curt Schilling—who has encyclopedic knowledge of, and intense appreciation for—baseball history, the game was particularly special. That's because Pittsburgh

37

star Roberto Clemente rapped out his three-thousandth hit, becoming just the eleventh major-league player to reach that milestone. The base hit would also be the last of Clemente's great career; later in the year he was killed in an airplane crash.

Although the young Curt Schilling admired Clemente and other good hitters, what he really loved was watching power pitchers like J.R. Richard, Nolan Ryan, and Tom Seaver. "I always liked power pitchers as all kids do," Schilling recalled. "I don't ever remember being excited about an offensive player in the game."[25]

Curt grew up playing Little League baseball. While he particularly enjoyed pitching, he was a good all-around athlete and also liked playing third base and hitting. Cliff Schilling encouraged his son and was an assistant coach on Curt's Little League teams.

As Curt grew older, he continued playing baseball and other sports. At Shadow Mountain High School, he pitched and played third base. Although not yet a standout player, he did show potential. The Cincinnati Reds displayed interest when Curt participated in a tryout camp after his junior year, but the Reds decided he was too young. When Curt was a senior, the Milwaukee Brewers scouted him, but after he broke his elbow during a summer league game, his hopes of being drafted evaporated.

Schilling decided to attend Yavapai Junior College in Prescott, Arizona. He made the Yavapai baseball squad and helped the Roughriders compete in the 1985 Junior College World Series. "We were the No. 1 junior college team in the nation," recalled Schilling. "It was one of the greatest, most fun years of my life."[26]

Road to the Major Leagues

Schilling's college performance caught the eye of big-league scouts, and in January 1986 he was drafted by the Boston Red Sox. After signing with the team for $20,000, Schilling was sent to the minor leagues to hone his pitching skills. But with his newfound independence he developed a taste for partying. "I went from Yavapai Junior College to professional baseball," he said. "I expected to be told how to walk, how to talk, how to do everything. But it wasn't that way. . . . I had so much fun. And got in so much trouble."[27]

In January 1988, Cliff Schilling died of a brain aneurysm. Curt Schilling had always looked up to his father, and he was devastated by the news. As a way to deal with his grief, Schilling began to leave a ticket in Cliff's name at the box office every time he pitched. Knowing his father's empty seat was out there helped him to focus on that day's game. Schilling has continued this tradition in the hundreds of major-league games in which he has pitched throughout his career.

Schilling made his first major-league appearance in 1988, but not with the Red Sox. In July, while he was playing in the minors, Boston traded him to Baltimore. At the end of the 1988 season, the Orioles called Schilling up to the major leagues. He started four games but was ineffective. Schilling spent most of the next season in the minors, joining the Orioles again in September 1989. This time he made a start and four relief appearances, posting a record of 0-1 and a bloated earned run average of 6.23.

Schilling spent all of 1990 with the Orioles. He appeared in thirty-five games as a reliever, posted his first major-league victory, saved three games, and had a solid 2.54 earned run average. Despite this improvement, the Orioles traded him to the Houston Astros after the season.

Schilling reported to spring training with the Astros in 1991 and won the job as the team's closer. But he was not successful in that role, and he missed his girlfriend, Shonda Brewer, who still lived in Baltimore. Eventually, the Astros sent Schilling down to their minor-league team in Tucson to work on his pitching mechanics. Schilling was determined to return to the big-league club, and he earned his chance later in the season. By the end of the 1991 season he had appeared in fifty-six games for Houston, posting a 3-5 record and a 3.81 ERA.

A Wake-Up Call

Schilling prepared for the 1992 season by working out in the weight room at the Astrodome. One day, he happened to be hitting the weights at the same time as superstar Red Sox pitcher Roger Clemens, a Texas native. Clemens asked to speak

Curt Schilling credits Roger Clemens (right) with encouraging him to become more serious about his pitching in a conversation before the 1992 season.

with Schilling. It was a conversation that would change the young pitcher's life.

"I'm thinking, 'Cool, he's one of my heroes. He wants to say hi,'" recalled Schilling. "About an hour and 15 minutes later . . . I walked back to the other side of the weight room. . . . He told me I was wasting my career, and I was cheating the game. And you know what? He was right. . . . It was no accident my career turned around immediately after that."[28]

Clemens's tongue-lashing had an immediate impression on Schilling, and he decided to work harder to make the most of his talent. But the Astros would not be the beneficiaries of Schilling's new outlook. In early April, he was traded to the Philadelphia Phillies for pitcher Jason Grimsley.

The Phillies finished last in the National League East in 1992, but they were a rebuilding team. Curt Schilling spent part of the season pitching from the bullpen, but he eventually moved into a starting role. He ended up with a 14-11 record, a 2.35 ERA, ten complete games, and 147 strikeouts. Many observers—including Clemens—were impressed at his improvement. "You can talk to somebody all you want, but unless they take the advice and run with it the way Curt did, it's a waste," said Clemens. "I have a smile on my face every time I see him going out there and doing what he's doing."[29]

The Magical 1993 Season

In 1993 everything seemed to come together. Before the start of the baseball season, Curt Schilling married Shonda Brewer. When the season got under way, the Phillies immediately began scratching and clawing their way to victories. Philadelphia fans fell in love with their scruffy but scrappy team, led by veterans John Kruk, Darren Daulton, and Lenny Dykstra. They did not look pretty, but they knew how to win. Schilling fit in well with his teammates, and he was happy with the way he was pitching.

The Phillies went from worst to first in the National League East, finishing 97-65 to reach the playoffs for the first time in ten years. Schilling was a major contributor. He compiled a 16-7 record, with seven complete games and 186 strikeouts.

Schilling was on the mound for the first game of the National League Championship Series (NLCS) on October 6, 1993, against the Atlanta Braves. He pitched a strong game, leaving the game in the ninth inning with the score tied. The Phillies went on to win the game in the tenth. The Phillies lost games two and three, but tied the best-of-seven series by winning game four. Schilling started game five; again he lasted into the ninth inning and left with the game tied. And once again the Phillies rallied to win in the tenth. When Philadelphia won the sixth game, the Phillies were headed to the World Series. Schilling was named Most Valuable Player of the NLCS for his outstanding efforts in games one and five.

The Phillies' magic dissipated in the World Series against the defending champion Toronto Blue Jays. After losing three of the first four games, Philadelphia was one loss away from elimination when Schilling took the mound for game five on October 21, 1993, at Veterans Stadium. Schilling pitched a masterful five-hit shutout to win the game, 2-0, and keep his team's hopes alive. But Philadelphia's luck finally ran out in game six. The Phillies were leading by a run in the bottom of the ninth when Toronto's Joe Carter hit a three-run homer to win the game and the World Series.

Years of Frustration

Before the 1994 season, baseball underwent major changes. The National and American Leagues were reorganized from two to three divisions, and the playoff format was expanded to include a wild-card team. The 1994 season was an exciting one for baseball, as several players were having potentially record-breaking seasons statistically. Unfortunately, the season ended in August because of a strike by the players, and the World Series was ultimately cancelled.

Schilling started 1994 as Philadelphia's staff ace, but a series of injuries—he pulled a tendon in his foot, had a bone spur removed from his elbow, and hurt his knee getting out of a chair—limited him to just thirteen games. He finished with a disappointing 2-8 record, including seven straight losses, and ended the season rehabbing in the minor leagues at Scranton.

In 1995 Schilling was again the team's opening-day starter. However, he was still not the same pitcher he had been two years earlier. His arm did not feel right. Doctors found that Schilling had a torn muscle and a bone spur in his shoulder. After an operation repaired the damage, Schilling dedicated himself to a comeback. Rehabilitation during the off-season helped him pitch better in 1996. Although he finished with a record of 9-10, he led the league in complete games with eight. With the retirement or departure of several older players, Schilling also emerged as a team leader.

He would be leading an awful team in 1997. By July 27, the Phillies were 30-72 and were on pace to lose more than one hundred games. One of the few bright spots was Schilling, who was having his finest season and was selected to the National League All-Star team for the first time. Although the Phillies

Schilling, on the mound for the Phillies, fires a pitch during a 1997 game.

rallied in the second half of the season, they still finished with a pathetic 68-94 record. Schilling posted a solid 17-11 mark with a 2.97 earned run average and seven complete games. He led the league in strikeouts for the first time, with 319. This set a National League record for strikeouts by a right-handed pitcher, breaking the old mark set by J.R. Richard in 1979. Schilling finished fourth in the balloting for the 1997 Cy Young Award.

Over the next two seasons, he continued to win games and pitch well for bad teams. He ended 1998 with a 15-14 record and again led the league in complete games (fifteen) and strikeouts (three hundred). Schilling became just the fifth pitcher in baseball history to strike out three hundred batters in consecutive seasons. He was on pace for an even better year in 1999, with a 15-6 record and eight complete games, but another arm injury cut his season short.

A Welcome Change

Schilling had blossomed into one of the best pitchers in the National League, a status confirmed by two straight appearances in the All-Star Game. But he was frustrated at the Phillies' losing ways, and he publicly blamed the team's owners for not being committed to putting together a winning team. His negative remarks were often quoted by sportswriters, and by July 2000 Philadelphia's management had had enough. Schilling was traded to Arizona for four players.

Schilling quickly became friendly with Arizona ace Randy Johnson, who had joined the team as a free agent before the 1999 season. Though physically very different, the two players had a lot in common—both were power pitchers and fierce

After years of playing with underachieving teams in Philadelphia, Schilling was excited to don the Diamondbacks' uniform late in the 2000 season.

competitors. Luis Gonzalez began referring to them as the "Odd Couple," and the nickname stuck. Schilling credits Johnson with helping him become a better pitcher. This was not obvious at first, though; Schilling managed just a 5-6 record with the Diamondbacks during the second half of the season.

In 2001 Schilling and Johnson became an unstoppable pitching force. Schilling went 5-1 in May to win Pitcher of the Month honors. Not only was he selected to the All-Star team (for the fourth time), he was also picked to be the National League's starting pitcher—a great honor. However, Schilling had pitched just before the All-Star break, and he did not want to throw with a tired arm and perhaps jeopardize his next start with the Diamondbacks. He asked that Johnson, also an All-Star, pitch in his place. To many people, this proved Schilling had become a true team leader. "That showed me, and everyone else, that his first concern was the Diamondbacks," said Luis Gonzalez. "That was a pretty prestigious honor he gave up."[30]

On September 5, 2001, Schilling became the first player in franchise history to win twenty games in a season. Less than a week later, with the Diamondbacks close to clinching their division, the season was interrupted by the tragic September 11 terrorist attacks. Schilling wrote an emotional letter that summed up his thoughts on sports and their place in society. To the families of firefighters and policemen killed in the terrorist attacks, he wrote, "Please know that athletes in this country look to your husbands and wives . . . as heroes, as idols, for they are everything every man should strive to be in life."[31]

World Series Heroics

After the baseball season resumed, the Diamondbacks finished with a 92-70 record, earning the right to play the St. Louis Cardinals in the division series. Schilling was Arizona's game one starter, and he dominated, pitching a complete-game, three-hit shutout. Schilling again took the mound for game five. He permitted just one run—the first he had given up in twenty-five consecutive postseason innings—and won when Tony Womack stroked an RBI single to break a 1-1 tie. The Diamondbacks won the division series and moved on to the National League Championship Series.

As in 1993, Schilling and his team would have to beat the Braves to reach the World Series. Schilling was the starter in game three, and he had another strong performance, striking out twelve batters and allowing just one run to give Arizona a two-games-to-one lead in the NLCS. "I can't believe what he's doing," commented Braves hitting coach Merv Rettenmund after the game. "He's throwing pitches we didn't even have in our book. He's making up pitches out there."[32]

The Diamondbacks beat the Braves in five games to earn a trip to the World Series. It was Schilling's turn to pitch as the Diamondbacks faced the New York Yankees in game one on October 27, 2001. He hurled seven solid innings as Arizona won easily, 9-1.

Arizona and New York split the next two games, and Schilling was called, on only three days' rest, to pitch in game four. Schilling again came through. He gave up just three hits and one run in seven innings, striking out nine batters. When Schilling left the game, Arizona had a 3-1 lead and seemed to be on the way to a commanding series lead. However, reliever Byung-Hyun Kim surrendered a game-tying home run in the ninth inning, and the Diamondbacks lost in the bottom of the tenth.

Arizona sustained another heartbreaking loss in game five, giving New York a three-games-to-two series lead. But Arizona was not finished. The Diamondbacks won the sixth game to tie the series. Schilling would be on the mound for the crucial seventh game. His opponent was the ace of the Yankees' staff, Roger Clemens, who ten years earlier had changed the course of Schilling's career with a stern lecture. Both stars pitched well. Clemens lasted six and one-third innings, giving up a run while striking out ten batters. Schilling pitched six shutout innings, but gave up single runs in the seventh and eighth before Arizona manager Bob Brenly took him out of the game. "You're my hero, big man," Brenly told Schilling, who was disappointed to have given up the go-ahead run. "That ain't going to beat us."[33]

Brenly was right. Randy Johnson shut down the Yankees in relief, and in the bottom of the ninth the Diamondbacks scored twice to win the World Series.

Schilling and Randy Johnson hold World Series trophies during a ceremony after the Diamondbacks' game seven win. The two star pitchers were named co-MVPs of the 2001 World Series.

After the game, Schilling and Johnson were named co-MVPs of the World Series for their gutsy pitching. Schilling had started three games and posted a 1.69 ERA. The two pitchers would later be named "Sportsmen of the Year" by *Sports Illustrated*. Schilling also was runner-up for the National League's Cy Young Award with a regular-season record of 22-6, a 2.98 earned run average, 293 strikeouts, and six complete games.

Excellence on and off the Field

Curt Schilling continued to be one of the best pitchers in the National League over the next few years. In 2002 he set a personal high for victories in a season with twenty-three, against

Schilling has become one of the National League's best pitchers because of his careful preparation for opposing batters. He is pictured here writing in his pitching notebook between innings of a 2002 game.

only seven losses. He also posted a 3.23 ERA and struck out 316 batters, marking the third time in his career that he had reached three hundred K's. Again, he finished second to Randy Johnson in balloting for the Cy Young Award.

Off the field, the Schilling family welcomed another member, Garrison, in June 2002. Curt and Shonda Schilling have three other children: son Gehrig (born in 1996), daughter Gabriella (born 1998), and son Grant (born 2000). The Schillings' oldest son is named for baseball legend Lou Gehrig, who starred with the New York Yankees during the 1920s and 1930s, but died before his thirty-eighth birthday from amyotrophic lateral sclerosis (ALS). More commonly known as Lou Gehrig's disease, ALS is a progressive, fatal neuromuscular disease; its victims gradually lose the ability to move, speak, swallow, and, eventually, breathe.

Schilling has long been involved in efforts to combat ALS, and he has raised more than a million dollars to fight the disease. The Curt and Shonda Schilling ALS Fund for Research and Patient Services provides funds to improve the quality of life for families affected by ALS. The Schillings are involved in other charitable efforts as well. In August 2002, after Shonda

Schilling survived an operation to remove malignant skin cancer, she founded the SHADE Foundation to raise awareness of skin cancer.

Schilling remains one of the game's best, and most hard-working, pitchers. His success is the result of countless hours of preparation. Schilling keeps track of his performances, and of the tendencies of the batters he will face, on a laptop computer. He even keeps notes on the way that different umpires call games. It is this dedication that has enabled him to win more than 160 games and strike out more than 2,500 batters during his career.

CHAPTER 4

Byung-Hyun Kim

When Byung-Hyun Kim entered the major leagues in 1999, the right-hander attracted attention as much for his Korean background as for his submarine pitching motion. "BK," as his teammates call him, has earned the respect of those he has played with and those he has played against for his dedication to the game. As a reliever with the Diamondbacks, he converted seventy-nine of ninety-nine save opportunities. Unfortunately, he is perhaps best remembered for two World Series games when he did *not* get the job done.

Submarine Delivery

Byung-Hyun Kim was born on January 21, 1979, in Gwangju, Jollanamdo Province, South Korea. His father was a martial arts teacher, and Kim grew up practicing tae kwon do. Kim also started playing baseball at an early age. When he was in the fourth grade, he received his first baseball glove from his father, who thought baseball would prevent his son from becoming a bully.

Kim continued to play baseball through high school. One of his classmates and teammates at Gwangju High School was

Korean-born pitcher Byung-Hyun Kim's sidearm delivery makes him difficult for opposing batters to hit.

Hee Seop Choi, who also would eventually play in the major leagues. When Kim was a sophomore, the school's baseball team won the Blue Dragon Pennant, the most prestigious high school tournament in Korea. Kim threw twenty-three innings, giving up just one run and striking out forty-three batters, and was chosen as the tournament's most valuable player.

After graduating from high school, Kim could have signed with a team in the Korean Baseball League. Instead he decided to attend school at Sungyungwan University, where he pitched for the baseball team. His unusual sidearm delivery made him an effective starting pitcher. Success at Sungyungwan

University led to his selection to South Korea's national base-ball team in 1997. One of his teammates on the national team was pitcher Chan Ho Park, who would become a star with the Los Angeles Dodgers.

In 1998, during a game between the South Korean and U.S. national teams, Kim impressed American scouts and fans by striking out fifteen batters. He also competed in the Asian Games that year, pitching and winning a semifinal contest that helped South Korea win the gold medal. According to reports, the president of South Korea exempted the members of the team from compulsory military service for winning the cham-pionship. "If you want to know what this guy's made of, there

When Kim pitched well early in the 2001 season for the Diamondbacks, he became the team's closer.

it is," Arizona manager Bob Brenly would later comment. "You want to be in a dugout or a foxhole? Now that's pressure."[34]

In recent years, players from Korea, Japan, and other Asian countries have been successful in the major leagues. Many teams have looked for prospects in Asia, and after the 1998 Asian Games, Kim was a hot commodity. The Arizona Diamondbacks won a bidding competition for the young free-agent pitcher by signing him to a four-year, $2.4 million contract in February 1999. The Diamondbacks were optimistic, but some baseball observers wondered about the signing. These observers believed that because Kim had no professional baseball experience, the Diamondbacks were taking an expensive gamble on an essentially unknown quantity.

A Live Arm

When Kim joined the Diamondbacks for spring training in 1999, Arizona's manager and coaching staff praised the young pitcher. Pitching coach Mark Connor described Kim's best pitch as "like a Frisbee-type slider, but it's hard. A lot of guys who throw [sidearm], their breaking balls are slow and soft. His is quick. He's as good as advertised."[35]

Even veteran players were impressed. "I don't know how he does it," exclaimed Matt Williams. "He's got [a pitch] that drops and one that rises. He's amphibious."[36]

Despite the praise, the coaches felt that the twenty-year-old Kim was not ready for the major leagues, so he was sent to the Diamondbacks' Class-AA farm team, the El Paso Diablos, for some seasoning. He would not spend much time with the Diablos, though. Kim appeared in just ten games, going 2-0 with a 2.11 earned run average and thirty-two strikeouts in twenty-one and a third innings. In late May, he was called up to the Diamondbacks.

On May 29, 1999, Kim made his first major-league appearance in a game against the New York Mets. He took the mound at Shea Stadium in the bottom of the ninth inning. Kim's mission was to protect a slim 8-7 Arizona lead while facing the heart of the Mets' batting order, but the young Korean was not intimidated. With the game on the line, he set down third baseman Edgardo Alfonzo and first baseman John Olerud before striking out catcher Mike Piazza to end the game and earn his first major-league save.

There were other pressures in addition to those that came from appearing in the late innings of close games. Kim, who was just learning how to speak English, had difficulty fitting in to the rowdy Diamondbacks clubhouse. He also felt constant pressure from a group of South Korean journalists, who followed him everywhere and reported his every move in Korean newspapers. "I felt so sorry for him," said pitcher Todd Stottlemyre. "To be here and have no one understand you or your culture? Man, that's tough."[37]

His teammates accepted the young pitcher, but his coaches had to change some of his habits. He was ejected from a June game against the Cubs when an ointment-covered bandage fell out of his shirt; the pitcher said that he had forgotten to take off the bandage before entering the game. Kim also earned the nickname "Lion" (after the song "The Lion Sleeps Tonight") for his ability to sleep anywhere and anytime. "You could put him in a chair and he could be asleep before you turn around,"[38] joked pitcher Mike Morgan. However, this occasionally got him in trouble with the coaches—for example, the time he fell asleep in the bullpen and had to be awakened in order to warm up during the late innings of one contest. "BK had to learn some things, like you can't fall asleep during a major league baseball game,"[39] commented bullpen coach Glen Sherlock.

Kim's performance on the field was spotty. He appeared in twenty-five games, going 1-2 with a 4.61 ERA and striking out thirty-one batters in twenty-seven and a third innings. However, because of his uneven performance the coaches decided he needed more work in the minors, and he was sent down to Class-AAA Tucson. There, Kim proved that he had no problem handling minor-league hitters. He appeared in eleven games with Tucson, going 4-0 with one save, a 2.40 ERA, and forty strikeouts in thirty innings pitched. He even started three games.

The Closer

At the start of the 2000 season, the Diamondbacks expected Matt Mantei to be their closer—the pitcher who would finish games for them. Mantei had saved thirty-two games in 1999. When spring-training injuries placed Mantei on the disabled list, twenty-one-year-old Byung-Hyun Kim was given the closer's job.

During the first half of the season, Kim was up to this important role. He threw his slider and fastball effectively, and posted fourteen saves and a 1.82 earned run average. Thanks to his success, he was even considered for the All-Star team. In mid-season, though, Kim went through a period of ineffectiveness and began to blow saves. When Mantei returned to the team, he assumed the closer's role, and Kim was sent back to Tucson for more work.

Kim comes off the mound to field a bunt during a 2003 game. Since reaching the major leagues in 1999, he has worked hard to make himself a solid all-around player.

"I think when he first got here, he had a sense that if anybody got a hit off him, he had failed," said Diamondbacks general manager Joe Garagiola Jr. "And if he lost a game, he was a complete failure."[40]

Kim was eventually recalled to the Diamondbacks and pitched from the bullpen, although he did get his first major-league start. He appeared in sixty-one games, finishing the season with a 6-6 record and a 4.46 earned run average. His performance was still spotty—he could be unhittable one night, but unable to get anybody out the next—yet he impressed observers by striking out 111 batters in just seventy and two-thirds innings. Although the Diamondbacks had a disappointing season in 2000 and missed the playoffs, Kim would be back in Arizona's bullpen for good.

A Major Contributor

In 2001 Mantei was again slated to be the team's closer, but he tore ligaments in his elbow after pitching in only eight games. For a time, Kim and Bret Prinz shared the closing duties. As Kim pitched effectively, and proved to be the better pitcher in that difficult role, he was given the job full-time.

Kim was a major contributor as the Diamondbacks won the National League West title. He appeared in seventy-eight games, compiling nineteen saves, a 5-6 record, and a 2.94 earned run average. He again averaged more than one strike-out per inning, with 113 K's over ninety-eight innings.

After winning the division title, the Diamondbacks faced the St. Louis Cardinals in the first round of the 2001 playoffs. Byung-Hyun Kim appeared in only one game during the series. Although he did not give up a run, and finished with a save, the numbers do not tell the whole story. Kim was wild and allowed two base runners in the ninth before nailing down the win.

"We tried to calm him by using as much Korean as we could, but my Korean was a little bit rusty," joked Mark Grace. "But, hey, I was trying to calm myself down, too."[41]

In the National League Championship Series, against the Atlanta Braves, Kim's pitching was flawless. He appeared in the second game and pitched a scoreless ninth in a non-save situation. He pitched the eighth and the ninth innings of game four to pick up a save, then pitched the eighth and ninth innings of game five for his second save. The Diamondbacks had won the National League championship, and Kim had not yielded a run in six and a third innings.

Meltdown

The Diamondbacks had a two-games-to-one lead in the World Series when Kim got his next call to save a game. Arizona held a two-run lead when Kim entered game four in relief of Curt Schilling. He was dominating in the bottom of the eighth, striking out all three batters he faced. After the Diamondbacks went out in the bottom of the ninth without scoring, Kim returned to the mound. He got the first two outs of the inning, then gave up a single. Facing the next batter, Tino Martinez, Kim threw a bad pitch that Martinez smacked over the fence for a game-tying two-run homer. Kim had blown the save opportunity.

The game went into extra innings and the Diamondbacks again failed to score in the top of the tenth. Kim stayed in the game for the bottom of the tenth. Again, he got the first two outs. This time, though, Derek Jeter hit a home run to give the

Kim is consoled by his manager and teammates after giving up a ninth-inning, game-tying homer to Scott Brosius in game five of the 2001 World Series.

Yankees an improbable 4-3 comeback win. Kim was charged with the loss, and the series was tied.

The next night, November 1, Arizona starter Miguel Batista and reliever Greg Swindell combined on eight innings of shutout baseball. With Arizona leading 2-0, Brenly called on Kim to preserve the lead in the ninth inning. "I called down to the bullpen to see how [BK] was warming up," Brenly later commented. "They told me his stuff was electric."[42]

It did not seem that way to the Yankees. Catcher Jorge Posada led off with a double. Kim struck out the next two batters, but then Scott Brosius hit a two-run homer to tie the game. Kim had let his teammates down for the second night in a row. Once again the Yankees won in extra innings, and they now held a three-games-to-two advantage for the series.

"I am so sorry to my teammates and my manager for giving up the tying run," Kim said through an interpreter after the game. "I want to thank my manager for giving me another chance to pitch."[43]

After Brosius's home run, several Arizona players came to the mound to encourage the disappointed young pitcher. "There's a lot of respect for BK in this clubhouse," said pitcher Todd Stottlemyre. "The way these guys put their arm around him showed that. They weren't going to let him be out there by himself."[44]

Kim watched from the bench, unable to contribute as Arizona won the sixth and seventh games to earn the World Series title. For Byung-Hyun Kim, the victory was bittersweet. His pitching throughout the season and during the playoffs had been invaluable, and without him the Diamondbacks might never have made it to the World Series. Still, his blown saves in the fourth and fifth games had almost lost the series for Arizona. He had a lot to think about during the off-season.

Back Where He Belonged

Before the 2002 season, many people wondered if Byung-Hyun Kim would ever be able to recover from his embarrassing ineffectiveness during the World Series. Kim assured his detractors that he would be fine. "I have tasted the worst part," he said. "I had all the confidence then, and I have more confidence now."[45]

Teammates, coaches, and friends also expressed their support for the reliever. "BK is always confident," explained his interpreter, Sung Cheul Ju. "He believes in the idea of *chi*. There is a balance of good and bad. BK believes the worst is behind him, and from here everything is good."[46]

This turned out to be correct in 2002. Kim again was the Diamondbacks' closer, and he pitched even better than he had in 2001. Appearing in seventy-two games, he recorded an 8-3 record, thirty-six saves, and a 2.04 earned run average. He struck out ninety-two batters in eighty-four innings pitched. Once again, his pitching was a major reason Arizona won the division title.

The first round of the 2002 playoffs featured a rematch of the 2001 National League Division Series between Arizona and St. Louis. The Cardinals were ready this time, however, and they swept the Diamondbacks in three games. In the final game, Kim suffered another disappointing outing. He entered the game in the eighth inning, with the Diamondbacks losing 4-3, and St. Louis nicked him for two more runs. When the Diamondbacks failed to score in the top of the ninth, their season was over. Although Kim had not done his job to keep the score close, the playoff loss was certainly not his fault. The Diamondbacks had an anemic .184 team batting average in the series.

Kim began the 2003 season with the Diamondbacks but was traded to the Boston Red Sox in May. He pitched well with the Red Sox—both as a starter and a reliever—collecting nine wins and sixteen saves with a respectable 3.34 ERA. Kim's contributions helped Boston reach the playoffs for the first time in four years.

By the end of the 2003 season, Byung-Hyun Kim had five years of major-league baseball under his belt. But he is young and still learning the difficult craft of pitching. For this hurler from South Korea, the best may be yet to come.

CHAPTER 5

Mark Grace

After reaching the major leagues in 1988, first baseman Mark Grace became one of baseball's best hitters. He collected more hits during the 1990s than any other player in the game. After thirteen seasons with the Chicago Cubs, he joined the Diamondbacks before the 2001 season and became a key member of the World Series–winning team. During his 16-year career Grace amassed 2,445 hits and boasted a lifetime batting average over .300. He was also a solid defensive player, winning four Gold Gloves.

Road to the Major Leagues

Mark Eugene Grace was born on June 28, 1964, in Winston-Salem, North Carolina. His family moved to several cities around the country but eventually settled in California, where Mark played various sports. His parents, Gene and Sharon Grace, were strict. They expected him to behave himself in school and on the playing field, and Mark grew up with a strong respect for teachers and coaches. "My parents taught me a lot of great things, but maybe the most important thing in terms of sports was that they taught me to listen to my

During his sixteen years in the major leagues, Mark Grace was one of the best hitters in baseball. He retired after the 2003 season with a career .303 batting average.

coaches," Grace later said. "As a kid, you think you're so smart, but no matter how smart you think you are, your coaches know more than you do and the best thing you can do for your own development is listen to them. They know more than you do."[47]

Mark began high school at Tustin High School in Tustin, California, not far from Los Angeles. He played baseball and basketball for the Tustin Tillers. After he graduated in 1982, he continued to play baseball, first at Saddleback College and then at San Diego State University. He played well enough to attract the attention of major-league scouts, and in 1985 the Chicago Cubs selected Grace in the twenty-fourth round of the draft.

After signing with the Cubs, Grace entered the minor leagues at Class-A Peoria in 1986. He excelled at Peoria, leading the league with a .342 batting average; he also hit fifteen homers and drove in ninety-five runs. The next season, 1987, he was promoted to Class-AA Pittsfield, where he led the league with 101 RBIs and posted a .333 batting average with seventeen home runs. This led to another promotion—he would start the 1988 season at Class-AAA Iowa.

Grace played only twenty-one games with Iowa before the Cubs brought him up to the majors. Chicago first baseman Leon Durham had been having trouble at the plate, and the Cubs wanted to see if Grace could handle the position. Grace excelled from the start, hitting .330 in his first month. The Cubs gave him the job on a full-time basis.

Durham, a benched veteran waiting to be traded, could have snubbed the young player who had taken over his position. Instead, Durham was kind and offered the rookie useful advice. "Leon Durham was really a good dude," Grace said later. "He

Grace smacks a two-run homer during a 1989 game. His hitting helped the Cubs win their division that year for just the second time in team history.

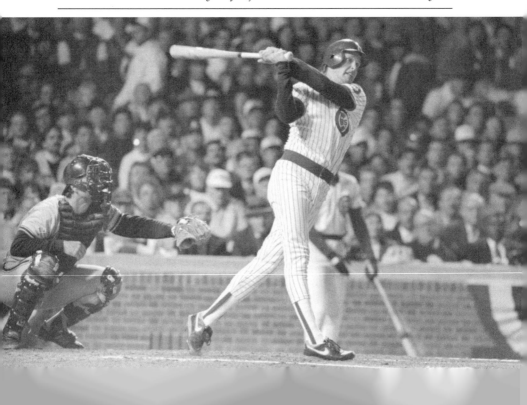

really helped me. He said that Bill Buckner had done the same thing for him in a similar situation, and now he was returning the favor."[48]

Durham was eventually traded to Cincinnati. Grace, meanwhile, had an opportunity to learn from other veteran Cubs stars like second baseman Ryne Sandberg, outfielder Andre Dawson, and pitcher Rick Sutcliffe. Grace finished the year hitting .296 with twenty-three doubles. But he had difficulties in the field, tying for the most errors among National League first basemen. Despite this, he finished second, to Cincinnati's Chris Sabo, in Rookie of the Year balloting for 1988.

Disappointments in Chicago

In 1989 Grace showed that his first season had not been a fluke. He posted an excellent .314 batting average, hit thirteen homers, and drove in seventy-nine runs. He also showed vast improvement in his fielding. He was an important piece of a Cubs team that won the National League East with a 93-69 record under manager Don Zimmer. It was only the second time that the Cubs had won the National League East Division.

The Cubs' last World Series appearance had come in 1945, so Chicago fans rooted excitedly for their team to win the National League Championship Series. It was not Chicago's year, however. The San Francisco Giants beat the Cubs four games to one in the series to take the league pennant. Grace had done about as much as he could for the Cubs during the series. He batted a blazing .647 with eight RBIs, and among his eleven hits were two doubles, a triple, and a home run.

Chicago fans enjoyed their team's success in 1989. Unfortunately, the club would not reach the playoffs again for nearly a decade. Between 1990 and 1997, Chicago managed winning records in just two seasons. Yet Grace continued to be a steady, solid performer both at the plate and in the field. He was recognized as the best defensive first baseman in the National League in 1992, 1993, 1995, and 1996, when he was awarded Gold Gloves for his play in the field.

At the plate he remained consistent as well. He followed up his fine 1989 season by batting .309 with nine home runs and eighty-two RBIs in 1990. Grace's average fell off somewhat, to

.273, in his fourth season, 1991, but he came back strong the next year to hit .309. He played even better in 1993, amassing 193 hits, including thirty-nine doubles and fourteen home runs, to post a career-best .325 batting average. He also drove in ninety-eight runs. Amazingly, although he had more than six hundred trips to the plate, he struck out just thirty-two times. That season, he was voted to the National League's All-Star team for the first time.

Grace was having a solid but not spectacular year in 1994, hitting .298, when the season ended in August because of a strike by the players. It had been an awful year for the Cubs, though, as they finished last in the division with a 49-64 record. The acrimonious strike not only shortened the 1994 season and forced the cancellation of the World Series, it also delayed the start of the 1995 season.

After the teams finally started playing ball again in 1995, Grace put together one of his finest all-around seasons. He batted .326, the fifth-best mark in the league, with sixteen home runs, ninety-seven runs scored, and ninety-two RBIs. Even though he played in only 143 games, he smacked a league-leading fifty-one doubles, becoming one of the few players in baseball history to hit more than fifty doubles in a season. He was third in the league in hits (180) and extra-base hits (70). Grace was selected to the All-Star team for the second time, and he won his third Gold Glove for his defense at first base. Behind his efforts the Cubs finished the 1995 season with a winning record of 73-71, but the team was still twelve games behind division-champ Cincinnati.

In 1996 Grace posted the best batting average of his career, .331, which again ranked him fifth among National League hitters. He followed that up with a thirteen-homer, .319 season in 1997, a year he was again selected for the All-Star team. However, the Cubs reverted to their losing ways, finishing 76-86 in 1996 and 68-94 in 1997.

Grace had proven that he was one of the best hitters in baseball, and he was a fan favorite because of his consistently solid play. The only problem was that the Cubs were not winning. Grace considered playing for another team, and at one point he even thought about making a move to the south side of

Chicago to play for the American League White Sox. He decided against the move, though, hoping the franchise would turn things around. In 1998 the Cubs did just that.

A Taste of Success

After the players' strike in 1994, which led to the cancellation of the World Series, many fans were disgusted with baseball. When the games started again in 1995, people stayed away from the ballparks. For the next few seasons, attendance remained down throughout the major leagues. It was not until 1998, when a fascinating race for the National League home-run title captivated the country, that many people tuned back into the game.

In 1961 a slugger named Roger Maris had set a major-league record by hitting sixty-one home runs in a season, breaking the mark of sixty set by Babe Ruth in 1927. No other player had

Grace congratulates Mark McGwire as the St. Louis slugger rounds the bases after hitting his record-breaking sixty-second home run in 1998.

ever hit sixty home runs in a season. But in 1997 Mark McGwire made a run at the record, finishing with fifty-eight homers. From the start of the 1998 season the St. Louis Cardinals' star first baseman was focused on breaking Maris's record. So, too, was one of Mark Grace's Chicago Cubs teammates: outfielder Sammy Sosa.

Throughout the season, Sosa and McGwire battled for the league home-run lead. Every day newspapers and television programs kept track of their progress toward the record. The race brought many fans back to baseball. McGwire was the first to break the record, homering in a September 8 game against the Cubs. Sosa remained close behind him in the home-run race throughout September. By the end of the season, McGwire had set a new record with an incredible seventy homers, while Sosa finished with sixty-six.

Sosa had an incredible season: He batted .308 and drove in 158 runs to win the league's Most Valuable Player Award. The Cubs also got good pitching from Kevin Tapani, who went 19-9, and Kerry Wood, who finished 13-6 and was voted the National League's Rookie of the Year. And Mark Grace chipped in with another solid season, hitting .309 with eighty-nine RBIs and career-best totals in home runs (seventeen) and runs scored (ninety-two). Thanks to their great performances, the Cubs finished with a 90-73 record and won the wild-card play-off spot.

More Woes in the Windy City

Unfortunately for baseball fans in the Windy City, the Cubs were no more successful in the first round of the 1998 playoffs than they had been in 1989. The powerful Atlanta Braves rolled over the Cubs, winning in three straight games. Chicago seemed to forget how to hit against the Braves' pitchers; Grace went just one for twelve (.083), although he did drive in one of the four runs the Cubs scored during the series; Sosa finished one for eleven (.182).

The Cubs reverted to form in 1999—they finished last in their division with a 67-95 record, thirty games out of first place. Sosa's sixty-three homers and Grace's .309 average and 107 runs scored were among the only bright spots in the dismal season.

But the 2000 Cubs were even worse, finishing 65-97. Grace, in the final year of his contract, struggled as well. Injuries— first a broken finger, then a pulled hamstring muscle—plagued him throughout most of the season. There were some high- lights—on August 6 he went five-for-five with two doubles and a home run against San Diego, and on September 23 he drove in his one-thousandth career RBI in a game against St. Louis—but on the whole the season was disappointing. Grace's batting average slipped to .280, the second-worst figure of his career. Despite this, he drove in eighty-two runs and proved that his eye was as good as ever by drawing ninety-five walks while striking out only twenty-eight times.

As the season drew to a close, the Cubs made it clear that the team would not offer Grace another contract. Management wanted to cut payroll, and Grace had earned $5.3 million in 2000. In the last weeks of the season, fans at Wrigley Field displayed signs supporting the popular first baseman, but it was no use. Chicago's front office chose to ignore the intangi- bles Grace brought to the Cubs, also overlooking the fact that his injuries had contributed to his subpar performance in 2000. They blamed Grace for the failed season and said he was washed up. Even though Grace had averaged .308 during his career with the Cubs, the team did not offer to extend his contract. "Never to make an offer is a little hurtful after 13 years," said his agent, Barry Axelrod. "He loves the ballclub and Chicago. . . . He deserved more."[49]

Chicago's loss turned into Arizona's gain when the infielder signed a contract with the Diamondbacks before the 2001 sea- son. Grace had spent many years on losing teams, so he was thrilled at the possibility of playing for a contender. Arizona had the core of a very good team and was hoping to return to the playoffs under new manager Bob Brenly. "It's an exciting feeling knowing that you're going to be on a good team, with a good pitching staff from top to bottom, and knowing you're going to contend," Grace said. "I have a chance to win again."[50]

Winning with Grace

Both Mark Grace and the Diamondbacks wanted to put the dis- appointing 2000 season behind them when 2001 began. Grace

After the Cubs decided not to offer Grace a contract, the first baseman signed with the Diamondbacks in December 2000.

started off strong. In a May 22 game against the rival San Francisco Giants, he had four hits as Arizona won, 12-8. The Diamondbacks erased memories of their third-place finish by winning the division in 2001, and Mark Grace was a big part of their success. He finished with a .298 batting average, fifteen home runs, and seventy-eight RBIs. And, as usual, he played solid defense at first base.

In the playoffs, Grace exorcised the demons of 1998 by hitting .375 as the Diamondbacks beat St. Louis, then Atlanta, to capture their first pennant. Grace was thrilled to have reached the World Series and excited to face the New York Yankees. "I've never been to Yankee Stadium," he said. "I've never played the Yankees all these years. I've always been in the National League, and, believe it or not, the Cubs have never played the Yankees in the postseason."[51]

The night before the first game of the World Series, Grace could not sleep because he was so excited. He came to Bank One Ballpark hours before the first pitch. That night, Grace found out what playing in a World Series game was like. As he stood on the third-base line, he admitted to goose bumps during the National Anthem. "'The rockets' red glare'—that's when it really hit me," he said. "I thought, you know what? This is pretty exciting. . . . it was a better feeling that I ever, ever imagined."[52]

Grace ended up batting .263, with a double and a home run, in the World Series. Of his five hits, the most important came in the ninth inning of the seventh game. With the Diamondbacks

---

Grace hits a solo home run during game four of the 2001 World Series. Later in the series he would come through with a clutch single that sparked the Diamondbacks' ninth-inning game-seven rally.

trailing by a run in the bottom of the ninth, Grace led off with a base hit. Brenly signaled for a pinch runner to replace him on the base paths, and the hometown crowd cheered Grace for starting the rally as he left the game. He watched the rest of the action from the dugout as Arizona rallied to tie the game on Tony Womack's RBI double, then win the series on Luis Gonzalez's bloop single. Grace and his teammates erupted from the dugout to celebrate their improbable victory. They had proven their doubters wrong. Grace himself felt vindication. After being rejected by Chicago, he had proven that he could still play.

The Future

Grace's role with the team diminished in 2002. He was relegated to the part of a bench player, although he did share time

In addition to being an excellent hitter, Grace worked hard to become a solid defensive first baseman, winning four Gold Gloves during his career.

at first base with Erubiel Durazo. Offensively, he had his worst season, hitting just .252.

The thirty-nine-year-old re-signed with the team in 2003, but again his role was limited. He struggled to hit .200, and his biggest contribution to the Diamondbacks in 2003 may have been the mentoring he gave to prospect Lyle Overbay.

Before Arizona's final series of the year, against the St. Louis Cardinals, Grace announced that he would retire at the conclusion of the season. But he still had a little magic left in his bat. In his last start, the veteran thrilled a hometown crowd at Bank One Ballpark by stroking a double and a single in three at bats. In the sixth inning, when manager Bob Brenly replaced Grace with a pinch runner, the Arizona fans rose to their feet to give the first baseman a thunderous ovation. They, like baseball lovers everywhere, recognized Mark Grace's long commitment to excellence. Over the course of his sixteen-year career, Grace earned a reputation as a dedicated team player who was always ready to do what it took to win. With a lifetime batting average of .303, including 511 doubles among his 2,445 career hits, the chances are good that he will one day be inducted into the Baseball Hall of Fame.

In the meantime, with his playing days over, Grace looked forward to spending more time with his wife, Tanya, and their two young children as he mulled over his future. One possibility was a job in the broadcast booth; he had already worked as an analyst for ESPN during several playoff series. Rumors also circulated that Grace would like to land a coaching position in the Diamondbacks' organization. Whether or not his future includes coaching or managing, Mark Grace's reputation as an old-school baseball star remains secure.

CHAPTER 6

Matt Williams

Matt Williams is sometimes called the "original Diamond-back" because he was the first marquee player signed by the franchise. He was a five-time All-Star, a four-time Gold Glove winner for his stellar play at third base, and the American League's home-run champ in 1994. Williams was not a flashy player; instead, he chose to be a leader, and his solid play was the result of hard work and dedication. He retired during the 2003 season with 378 career home runs.

Quiet Determination

Matthew Derek Williams was born on November 28, 1965, in Bishop, California. While he was growing up in California and Nevada, he played baseball and other sports. He attended high school in Carson City, Nevada, where he played baseball for the Senators. Carson High School has a very good baseball program; other former Senators who have reached the major leagues include Bob Ayrault, Donovan Osbourne, and David Lundquist.

After graduating from high school in 1983, Williams was drafted by the New York Mets. However, he decided that he

Power-hitting third baseman Matt Williams retired in 2003 with 378 career home runs.

was not ready for professional ball. Instead, he enrolled at the University of Nevada–Las Vegas. At UNLV, Williams starred for the baseball team from 1984 to 1986. As a freshman he hit .322 with twelve home runs. The next season, he batted .311 and pounded twenty-one homers. These performances earned Williams a spot on the U.S. national team, and he played with the squad in Asia in 1985.

Williams had a fantastic junior year in 1986. The shortstop played in fifty-seven games for the Rebels and hit .351 with twenty-five homers and eighty-nine RBIs. He was selected as an All-American that year by such publications as *Baseball America*, the *Sporting News*, and *Collegiate Baseball*.

That would be his last season at UNLV. On June 7, 1986, the twenty-year-old Williams was the third player chosen in the major-league draft. He signed with the team that had selected him, the San Francisco Giants, and was sent to the minor leagues to begin his professional career. Even though he would not return to the Rebels for his senior year, Williams had set a school record with his fifty-eight career home runs, and UNLV honored him by retiring his number (15) and electing him to the school's hall of fame.

Williams did not spend much time in the minors. On April 11, 1987, he made his major-league debut. That season, he played in eighty-four games with the Giants. Fans could have had no idea from his statistics—a .188 batting average with eight home runs—that they were watching a future star.

A Rising Star

In 1988 and 1989 Williams split time between the Giants and their minor-league teams. Although he didn't hit particularly well in either year, he did gain valuable experience both at the plate and at third base. In 1989 he proved that he had some pop in his bat by hitting eighteen home runs—the third-highest figure on the team—in just eighty-four games. That season was special as the Giants won the National League West with a 92-70 record. First baseman Will Clark and left fielder Kevin Mitchell were the team's offensive stars; Clark had twenty-three homers and a .333 batting average, while Mitchell pounded forty-seven homers and hit .291.

In the National League Championship Series, the Giants defeated the Chicago Cubs in five games behind the hitting of Clark, Mitchell, and Williams. During the series Williams batted .300 with two home runs and nine RBIs, helping San Francisco reach the World Series for the first time in twenty-seven years.

Thirsty for a championship after the long drought, giddy Giants fans had another reason to be excited about the 1989 World Series: The American League pennant winners were the Athletics, whose home was in Oakland, right across San Francisco Bay. On October 14, the Bay Area rivals squared off in Oakland for game one of the much-anticipated series. To the dismay of the Giants' faithful, the A's rode shutout pitching from Dave Stewart and homers from Dave Parker and Walt Weiss to a first-game victory. Oakland won the next game, 5-1, to take a two-games-to-none lead as the series shifted to San Francisco for game three.

But as fans were filing into Candlestick Park before the third game, something extraordinary happened—an earthquake rocked San Francisco. No one in the stadium was injured, but the quake caused major damage throughout the Bay Area and led to more than 60 deaths. The World Series was postponed until October 27 because of the disaster.

When the series resumed, the A's picked up where they had left off, capturing the next two games for a World Series sweep. Williams had not hit the ball well, but neither had anyone else on the Giants.

Reasons for Optimism

Although the World Series loss was disappointing, Williams expected to be back again soon. But as it turned out, eight years would pass before he got another shot at a world championship. "You know, at the time you just don't appreciate how special it is,"[53] he later commented.

In 1990 Williams played his first full season with the Giants. He showed amazing improvement at the plate and was selected to the All-Star team for the first time in his career. By the time the season had ended, he had collected a National League–best 122 RBIs, smacked thirty-three home runs (fourth

Matt Williams starred for the San Francisco Giants from 1989 to 1996. In addition to hitting for power, he was excellent defensively at third base.

in the league), and posted a respectable .277 batting average. As a result of his fine offensive performance, Williams finished sixth in the balloting for the National League's Most Valuable Player Award.

The next season, he upped his home-run total to thirty-four, but he also shone in the field, winning his first Gold Glove at third base. His solid defense and exciting offense endeared Williams to Giants fans, as did his easygoing, understated manner.

Williams suffered through a disappointing 1992 season. His batting average fell to .227 and his home-run total dropped to twenty.

He bounced back in 1993, though. In addition to capturing his second Gold Glove, he posted big offensive numbers, including a .294 batting average and thirty-eight home runs (both new career bests). His 110 RBIs ranked fifth in the league, and he was also among the league leaders in slugging percentage (.561), extra-base hits (seventy-five), and total bases (325). After the season, Williams again finished sixth in the voting for Most Valuable Player.

Disappointment

The 1994 season may have been Williams's best; it was certainly his most exciting. From opening day on, he hit home runs at a prodigious pace, and sportswriters felt that he had a chance to break Roger Maris's single-season record of 61. By the end of June, Williams had socked twenty-nine homers, more than any National League player had ever hit by that point in a season. By the end of July, he had hit forty homers to establish another National League mark, and he remained on pace to break Maris's record.

In mid-August, however, major-league baseball players went on strike. When the players and the owners failed to come to an agreement, the remainder of the season was cancelled. Williams had a league-leading forty-three homers to his credit, but the chance to claim one of baseball's most prestigious records was gone. Another Gold Glove and a second-place finish in the MVP balloting hardly made up for this lost opportunity.

The strike delayed the start of the 1995 season and shortened it to 145 games. Because of a broken foot, Williams's season was even shorter. But in just seventy-six games he managed to hit twenty-three home runs, and he garnered All-Star honors for the third time. For his team, however, there was not much to cheer about: Without the services of their standout third baseman, the Giants finished dead last in the National League West.

In 1996 Williams made the All-Star team for the fourth time, but once again his season ended prematurely. This time he left the team in August for shoulder surgery. Playing in 105 games, the thirty-year-old star had hit twenty-two home runs and batted .302. However, the Giants once again finished in the basement of their division.

San Francisco fans expected Williams to bounce back for the 1997 season—but they never expected him to do so for another team in a different league. On November 13, 1996, the Giants traded Williams to the Cleveland Indians for Jeff Kent, Jose Vizcaino, and Julian Tavarez. The Giants made the deal to cut their payroll; Williams, at $7 million a year, was just too expensive. While Cleveland fans were ecstatic, San Francisco's faithful seethed. They lambasted Giants general manager Brian Sabean for making the trade. "All of a sudden I've gone from a golden boy to an idiot,"[54] Sabean remarked.

An Indian

In 1997, with Williams at third, Cleveland won the American League Central Division. Both at the plate and in the field, Williams was a key contributor to the Indians' success. He swatted thirty-two home runs and piled up 105 RBIs, and his stellar defensive play won him his fourth Gold Glove Award.

From his solid play on the diamond, it might have appeared that everything was going well for Matt Williams. In reality, his personal life was in turmoil. During spring training Michelle Williams had told her husband that she wanted to end their eight-year marriage. The divorce proceedings played out during the 1997 season, and Williams, a devoted father, was concerned about the impact on his children, Rachel, Jacob, and Alysha.

The Williamses were ultimately granted joint custody of their children, who traveled by airplane from Phoenix to Cleveland to be with their father during every Indians home series. The airplane travel and the separation upset both Matt Williams and his children. As a result, his mind simply was not on the game as much as it had been in the past. "Being there for my kids is everything in my life," Williams would later admit. "I'm a dad first and a baseball player second."[55]

Despite his trouble focusing on baseball during the 1997 season, Williams would go to the World Series for the second time in his career. The Indians beat the Yankees in the American League Division Series, three games to two, then took the American League pennant by defeating Baltimore in six games. The Indians were going to the World Series to play the Florida

Marlins, an expansion team that had entered the big leagues in 1993 and had reached the World Series faster than any expansion team to that point in baseball history.

Williams did his best to bring a crown to Cleveland, batting .385 in the seven-game series. But Florida prevailed in extra innings of the final game to upset the Indians and win the championship. The Indians were stunned by the loss, and no one was more disappointed than Williams. He told his friend and agent Jeff Moorad that he felt like quitting the game because of the tough loss and his family situation. Ultimately, Williams and Moorad decided that the best course would be for the third baseman to play for the new Arizona franchise, which would play its first season in 1998. This would allow Williams to be closer to his children.

"I remember reading an article in *Baseball Weekly* [about] how unhappy he was because of the separation with his kids," Diamondbacks general manager Joe Garagiola Jr. recalled. "So during the '97 World Series, I went to [Cleveland general

---

Williams slides home safely in game four of the 1997 World Series. The third baseman was devastated when Cleveland lost the series to the Florida Marlins in seven games.

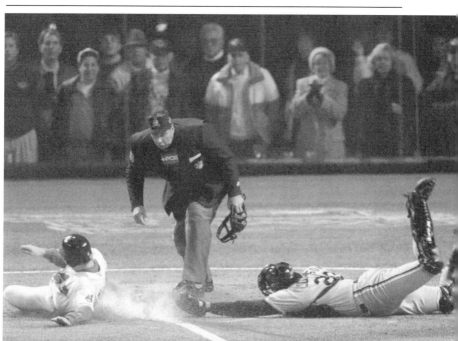

manager] John Hart's office and said, . . . will you trade Matt Williams? John told me, 'if it was anybody else but [Arizona] asking, I'd say no. But Matt would like to play there. And I would do it not because of a baseball dimension, but because of the human dimension. And Matt Williams is the finest person I know in baseball.'"[56]

At Williams's request, during the off-season the Indians traded him to the Diamondbacks for Travis Fryman, Tom Martin, and $3 million. Williams contributed $2.5 million of his own salary to make the deal happen.

The Original Diamondback

Williams was happy to be playing in Arizona, where he could be near his children. He put his personal troubles behind him and started dating a woman named Michelle Johnson. On the field, Williams assumed the role of team leader. However, he did not hit particularly well, batting just .267 with twenty home runs and seventy-one RBIs. And the team finished in last place with a 65-97 record.

"It was fun being on a team playing its first game in history, but we didn't win a whole lot of games," said Williams. "That made it tough."[57] Going from a club that reached the World Series to a last-place team might have been frustrating, but Williams's personal life was getting better. On January 15, 1999, he married Michelle Johnson.

The 1999 season saw an impressive turnaround for the Diamondbacks. The club finished in first place in the National League West. Williams was a big part of the team's success. He finished with thirty-five home runs and a .303 batting average, and he was voted to the All-Star team for the fifth time. At the end of the season Williams finished third in the voting for National League MVP. He had evolved into a true team leader and felt totally content in Arizona.

Williams continued to play well in the postseason. He batted .375 against the New York Mets, but it was not enough. The Diamondbacks lost the series in four games.

In 2000 injuries once again shortened Williams's season. This time a broken foot limited him to ninety-six games. He batted .275 with just twelve home runs and forty-seven RBIs. The

Although he struggled at the plate in the 2001 playoffs, Williams came through several times in the World Series. Here he watches a three-run homer leave the park during the second game.

Diamondbacks also had a disappointing season, finishing third in the National League West. But better days were ahead for the team.

In 2001 the Diamondbacks finished first in their division with a 92-70 record. Williams was consistent when he played, but he appeared in just 106 games, batting .275 with sixteen homers and sixty-five RBIs. In the first round of the playoffs, Arizona beat the Cardinals. Williams was no help in this series; he was just one for sixteen (.063) at the plate, with his only hit coming in the fifth game. He did better at the plate in the National League Championship Series, hitting .278 with four RBIs as Arizona beat the Braves. However, the normally sure-handed fielder committed three errors and was booed by Arizona fans.

In his third trip to the World Series, Williams redeemed himself for his poor performances earlier in the playoffs. After the Diamondbacks won the first game against the Yankees, Williams hit a three-run homer to win the second game. He finished the series with a .269 batting average and a team-leading seven RBIs as Arizona won the championship faster than any expansion team in history. After several close misses, Williams was a world champion. During the excitement of the celebration, former baseball player Joe Black, who had been Rookie of

After several years of declining productivity, Williams was released by Arizona during the 2003 season, and he decided to retire.

the Year in 1952, visited the Arizona clubhouse and spoke to Williams. "I told him that he's the reason why the Diamondbacks are champions," said Black. "He's taken a lot of bashing, a lot of criticism. But look who's standing?"[58]

A Stand-Up Guy

The World Series was the final moment of glory for Williams. Injuries limited him to just sixty games in 2002, during which he hit twelve homers and drove in forty runs. During the off-season, the Diamondbacks discussed trading the aging third baseman to the Colorado Rockies for Larry Walker, but both players vetoed the deal. At the start of the 2003 season, Williams continued to struggle; in May the Diamondbacks traded Byung-Hyun Kim to Boston for All-Star third baseman Shea Hillenbrand. The next month, Arizona released Williams, who had just four home runs, sixteen RBIs, and a .241 average in forty-four games. The thirty-seven-year-old decided to retire rather than try to sign with another team and disturb his family life again. "My kids are 13, 12, and 10, and I've been a baseball player and missed a lot of their time," he said. "It's more important to be present with them."[59]

Williams left the game with 378 home runs, 1,218 RBIs, a .268 career batting average—and the respect of practically everyone involved with major-league baseball. "He was a good player, a good teammate, and good friend,"[60] commented his former Giants teammate Barry Bonds.

But Arizona teammate Mark Grace perhaps best expressed the way others in the game felt about the classy infielder when he said, "I hope my son grows up to be like Matt Williams."[61]

CHAPTER 7

Luis Gonzalez

During his first eight full seasons in the major leagues, Luis Gonzalez never hit more than fifteen homers or drove in more than seventy-nine runs in a season. Since joining the Diamondbacks in 1999, however, he has become one of the game's best power hitters. Although he is a fierce competitor, "Gonzo," as he is known by his teammates, is considered one of the nicest players in baseball and is involved with many charitable organizations.

Boyhood and Baseball

Luis Emilio Gonzalez was born on September 3, 1967, in Tampa, Florida. His parents were Cuban Americans, so Luis grew up speaking Spanish at home but English at school and when playing with his friends.

The Gonzalez family lived on the west side of Tampa in a close-knit Hispanic neighborhood. Tampa is a hotbed for baseball, and when Luis was a child he could see such Tampa natives as Steve Garvey, Wade Boggs, and Dwight Gooden play in the big leagues. Luis started playing the game when he was very young. "I always seemed to have a ball, a bat, or a glove in

Diamondbacks outfielder Luis Gonzalez is considered one of the nicest people in baseball, as well as one of the National League's best hitters.

my hands," he said. "But it wasn't until I was about five or six years old when I first started playing organized baseball."[62]

The boys of the neighborhood played ball all the time. In addition to organized Little League baseball, they played pickup baseball games. When there weren't enough players for a baseball game, Luis and his friends played corkball, a game that involved two people, a broomstick, and a homemade ball made from a cork. "We would put pennies on each end of the cork for weight and tape it up," Gonzalez explained. "Then you flick it and the other guy tries to hit it."[63]

Luis played Little League baseball against such future baseball stars as Gary Sheffield, Tino Martinez, and Derek Bell. One year he and Martinez played together on the same West Tampa Little League all-star team, but their team lost to another Tampa-area all-star team featuring Gary Sheffield. "The teams with Sheffield and Bell always knocked us off,"[64] recalled Gonzalez.

When Gonzalez entered Jefferson High School, he began to play baseball for the Jefferson Dragons under the eye of coach Emetrio "Pop" Cuesta. He played second base and hit .400 while teammate Martinez batted .533 and hit for power. "My job was just to try to get on base so Tino could drive me in,"[65] remembered Gonzalez. In their senior year, 1985, the Jefferson team was nationally ranked but lost to Miami High School, which won the state championship.

"Ball Was Everything"

Although in high school Gonzalez was a talented player with a positive work ethic, most scouts did not consider him a major-league prospect. Gonzalez, however, always believed in himself. "It was my dream. I know they tell you that you should have a backup plan but it was all I ever wanted to do," he later admitted. "When I listened to the old men in the coffee shops, I thought that if I worked hard and really applied myself, I really could make it to the majors."[66]

His family, especially his mother and grandmother, encouraged his dream of playing professional baseball. "Ball was everything in Tampa," Gonzalez commented. "The biggest baseball fans of all were probably my mom and grandmother. They'd drive me all over town to see the good players."[67] Luis became even closer to his mother and grandmother after his parents divorced during his senior year. He often credits his mother, Ame Silverstein, and grandmother with instilling the values he lives by today.

After graduating, Gonzalez and Tino Martinez went to different colleges. Martinez was scouted by many major-league teams but decided to attend the University of Tampa. Gonzalez was overlooked by scouts, but he was offered a scholarship to play baseball at the University of South Alabama.

Improving His Skills

At the University of South Alabama, Gonzalez played baseball and studied radio and television broadcasting. The school had a top-notch baseball program, run by coach Steve Kittrell, and many Jaguars have reached the majors, including Marlon Anderson, Mike Mordecai, and Jon Lieber.

After his first season of college baseball Gonzalez was named to *Baseball America's* All-Freshman team. He played three years of solid baseball for the Jaguars, in the process drawing the attention of big-league scouts. His hard work paid off when he was selected by the Houston Astros in the fourth round of the 1988 amateur draft.

After signing a contract with the Astros, Gonzalez was sent to the minor leagues. Over the next three years, he played with minor-league teams in Auburn, Asheville, Osceola, and Columbus. He hit the ball well wherever he was sent, batting .282 overall in the minors, but he was never a standout player. Because he was fundamentally solid, scouts viewed Gonzalez as

As a high-school player Gonzalez was overshadowed by teammate Tino Martinez, but he gained the attention of big-league scouts while playing for the University of South Alabama from 1986 to 1988.

a player who would not hurt a team, but they also felt that he was not talented enough to truly be a star in the major leagues.

Toward the end of his third season in professional baseball, on September 4, 1990, Gonzalez finally got the call from the Astros. He played twelve games, at third base and at first, for Houston during 1990.

At spring training the next year, he won a roster spot on the Astros as an outfielder. Over the course of the 1991 season, he hit .254, with thirteen home runs and sixty-nine RBIs—decent numbers for a rookie.

Gonzalez played the 1992, 1993, and 1994 seasons with Houston. His best season was 1993, when he appeared in 154 games, hitting .300 with fifteen home runs and seventy-two RBIs.

Changes

On November 12, 1994, a major change occurred in Luis Gonzalez's personal life: he married Christine Lehmann, whom he

Gonzalez slides into second base during a 1997 game. That year, the outfielder helped Houston win its division.

had met four years earlier at a charity event. Eight months later a major change would occur in Gonzalez's professional life, as Houston traded him to the Chicago Cubs. Gonzalez spent the next season and a half with the Cubs. In 1996 he hit .271, matching his career high with fifteen home runs and driving in a career-best seventy-nine runs. After that season, though, Chicago traded him back to Houston.

Although Gonzalez batted just .258 with ten homers in 1997, the Astros won the National League's Central Division with an 84-78 record. Houston's playoff hopes were quickly dashed by perennial favorite Atlanta, however. The Braves swept the Astros in three games, outscoring them nineteen to five. Gonzalez hit the ball well in his first postseason appearance, collecting four hits in twelve trips to the plate for a .333 average.

At the end of the 1997 season, Gonzalez became a free agent. He decided to switch leagues, signing a contract with the Detroit Tigers. The 1998 season would be his breakout year, in part because Gonzalez changed his hitting style by opening his stance in the batter's box. "Opening up my stance just helped me to see the ball with both eyes and helped me clear my hips on the inside pitch,"[68] he explained. Gonzalez also started a weight-training program during the off-season. The changes helped him at the plate; he hit .267 but reached new career-best figures in home runs (twenty-three), doubles (thirty-five), and runs scored (eighty-four).

While his hitting was changing for the better, his home life was becoming vastly more exciting. In June 1998 Christine Gonzalez gave birth to triplets—Alyssa, Jacob, and Megan. Gonzalez credits the children with focusing his life. "I used to stress myself out pretty bad," he said. "But when you come home and see three little faces who all want your attention, you realize what's really important. . . . I'd never want to short-change them."[69]

Confidence at the Plate

After the 1998 season, Gonzalez was traded back to the National League. This time, he went to Arizona, which sent outfielder Karim Garcia to Detroit. The Diamondbacks initially planned to platoon Gonzalez in the outfield with Bernard

Gilkey, but Gilkey developed vision problems and was unable to play. Gonzalez stayed in the lineup full-time and hit better than he ever had in his career. Early in the season, he compiled an amazing thirty-game hitting streak. The streak finally ended when he went hitless in a May 19, 1999, loss to the San Francisco Giants. Gonzalez came right back, however, getting a hit in the next game to start a twelve-game streak. With this success, said Gonzalez, "my confidence at the plate took off."[70]

His resurgence took many people by surprise. Gilkey's name was listed on the ballots for the 1999 All-Star team, so Arizona fans started a write-in campaign to get Gonzalez on the team. Thousands of fans sent in ballots with Gonzalez's name. Although he was not among the top vote-getters, in recognition of the great season he was having, National League manager Bruce Bochy named Gonzalez to the All-Star team for the first time in his career.

Gonzalez ended the season with a National League–leading 206 hits. His .336 average and forty-five doubles ranked him second in the league in both categories, and he was also among the league leaders in triples (nine), runs scored (112), and total bases (337). He also set new career highs with twenty-six homers and 111 RBIs.

The Diamondbacks played just as well as Gonzalez did, winning one hundred games to take the National League West. However, in their first postseason appearance, the Diamondbacks fell to the New York Mets, three games to one. Gonzalez had a decent series at the plate, going three for ten with a double, a home run, and two RBIs. Arizona rewarded Gonzalez for his great 1999 season by signing him to a three-year, $12.5 million contract.

Gonzalez fit in well with the Diamondbacks both on and off the field. He became actively involved in charity work in the Phoenix area. He worked with the Make-a-Wish Foundation, participated in children's baseball promotions with a local dairy, and started an education program called Kids Going Gonzo for School. He also participated in Sunday's Sidekicks, a program in which fifty children are randomly selected to meet and ask questions of their favorite Diamondbacks players. The sessions are televised on the ballpark's scoreboards.

Arizona teammates congratulate Gonzalez after a two-run homer. The outfielder has been a key contributor to the Diamondbacks' success.

"When I was growing up my mom was a schoolteacher, and whenever any athlete would come to school or something like that, I always saw kids get really excited about it," explained Gonzalez. "And I just figured that this was a good opportunity for me to step out and say 'Hey, I want to do this and have kids have something to look forward to when they come to the park.'"[71]

The 2000 season was much better for Gonzalez than it was for the Diamondbacks. In a game against the Astros on July 5, he became the first Diamondback player to hit for the cycle (getting a single, double, triple, and home run in the same game). On September 23 Gonzalez hit three-run homers in both games of a doubleheader against the San Francisco Giants; he drove in eight runs that day. He finished the season with a career-high thirty-one home runs and a .311 batting average, and for the first time he played in all 162 of his team's games.

He was once again among the league leaders in hits, doubles, and total bases. Although the Diamondbacks had struggled to a third-place finish, better days were ahead.

A Remarkable Season

Gonzalez started off hot in the 2001 season. He tied a major-league record by hitting thirteen home runs in the month of April, a feat that helped him win National League Player of the Month honors. He won the award again in June after batting .417 with twelve homers for the month. In one interleague game against the Kansas City Royals on June 8, he hit three home runs.

Behind his hitting and the team's strong pitching, the Diamondbacks were winning a lot of games. Gonzalez was voted to the All-Star team, joining his teammates Curt Schilling and Randy Johnson. Gonzalez thrilled fans with an impressive performance in the All-Star Game's Home Run Derby, which he won. Among his sixteen homers was a blast that was estimated to have traveled 440 feet. Gonzalez was gracious after beating such famed sluggers as Barry Bonds and Sammy Sosa. "I was so nervous about coming out there, this being my first Home Run Derby," he said. "I was just hoping I'd fare well out there—to hit one or two."[72]

Gonzalez was hitting home runs at a rate that in many seasons would have led the major leagues. In 2001, however, Bonds was having one of the greatest seasons in baseball history. He had hit thirty-nine home runs by the All-Star break, and he would finish the season with seventy-three, setting a new major-league record. Bonds set several other records in the process, including most walks and best slugging percentage. Yet even Bonds acknowledged the great season Gonzalez was having. "You can't compare what Luis has done with what I've done," Bonds said. "He's done a lot more. His team is in first place. And except for homers, his numbers are much better than mine."[73]

Gonzalez finished the season with a .325 average, fifty-seven home runs, 419 total bases, and 142 RBIs. He led the Diamond-backs in almost every offensive category—batting average, hits, RBIs, total bases, slugging percentage, on-base percentage, doubles, triples, walks, and home runs. In almost any other year, Gonzalez would have been named the league's Most Valuable Player; he finished third in the balloting for the award behind Bonds and Sosa, who also had a phenomenal season (.328 average, sixty-four home runs, and 160 RBIs).

A Dream Come True

After winning their second division title in three years with a 92-70 record, the Diamondbacks advanced to the World Series by beating St. Louis and Atlanta. In the first game of the series against the Yankees—a team that included his high-school teammate Tino Martinez—Gonzalez hit his first World Series homer, a two-run shot in the third inning. The homer gave Arizona the lead, and the Diamondbacks went on to win the game, 9-1.

After winning game two, the Diamondbacks traveled to New York, where they lost three straight games. During the third game, Gonzalez decided to play a softly hit ball on a hop instead of trying to make a diving catch. On the play a run scored to give the Yankees a 2-1 lead. Gonzalez did not make excuses when asked about the play later. "As an outfielder, you have a split second to decide," he said. "If I try to make the catch [and don't] two runs score."[74]

After the heartbreaking late losses in games four and five, the Diamondbacks exploded for fifteen runs to win game six. In the seventh game, Gonzalez came to the plate in the bottom of the ninth with the score tied and Jay Bell on third base. Yankees reliever Mariano Rivera, who had been almost unhittable in the postseason, fired the first pitch in for a strike. On the next pitch, Gonzalez singled past shortstop Derek Jeter to score Bell with the winning run.

"I was facing one of the best relievers in baseball," an excited Gonzalez said after the World Series victory. "So basically what I was trying to do was just make good contact. In any kid's dream, the ideal situation would be to hit a home run—that was just as exciting as hitting a home run."[75]

As champagne sprayed in the raucous Arizona locker room, Gonzalez put the victory into perspective: "We said from Day One our goal was not just to get to the World Series but to win

Gonzalez delivers his World Series–winning bloop single. The ninth-inning hit scored Jay Bell to win the seventh game and give Arizona its first world championship.

it and we believed we would—even going to the ninth inning. This is a dream come true. This team will not give up. We kept battling."[76]

The Face of the Diamondbacks

Since winning the World Series, Gonzalez has continued to play great baseball. In 2002 he was again voted to the All-Star team. He played in every game until August 14, when he sat out because of a strained rib cage, ending a streak of 446 consecutive games. Gonzalez was soon back in the lineup, but on September 23, he sustained a more serious injury in an outfield collision. The injury kept him out of the playoffs, and the Diamondbacks missed his bat in their three-game loss to St. Louis.

After four excellent years with Arizona, the team decided to sign Gonzalez to a three-year, $30 million contract extension just before the 2003 season began. "Gonzo is the face of the Diamondbacks," commented manager Bob Brenly. "With all due respect to Randy [Johnson] and Curt [Schilling] and the other players on the team, you travel around the league, and this is one of the most respected, most feared hitters."[77]

Team owner Jerry Colangelo agreed. "The trade that was made to bring Luis here was an all-time deal for us," he said. "Gonzo has become an icon."[78]

Gonzalez proved that he was fully recovered from his injury. In 2003 he made the All-Star team for the fourth time, and, in a season that saw the Diamondbacks struggle, Gonzalez had a fine individual year. He finished the season hitting .304 with twenty-six home runs and 104 RBIs. "He's the one constant we've had this year," said Brenly. "He plays every day, and he's the most consistent offensive performer we have. He's the guy most teams are going to be concerned with."[79]

A Nice Guy

While his time in Arizona has been particularly fun for Luis Gonzalez, he always tries to make things fun for the people around him. He is considered one of the nicest guys in baseball because he is always willing to sign autographs and answer questions from fans, and he makes an effort to remember staff members' names when the team visits different ballparks. Over the years he has donated both his time and money to charities. When Gonzalez signed his contract extension in 2003, he and his wife promised to donate $1 million to charity.

Even though Luis Gonzalez has become one of the best players in the National League, he remains a down-to-earth man who is grateful for the opportunity to play baseball. "I'm

Gonzalez cheers as the winning run scores in the 2001 World Series.

excited to have this Diamondback uniform on for years to come," he said after signing his contract extension. "My career basically turned around here in Arizona. The organization, the fans, everyone in the whole state has treated my family like we were part of the family here. The fit is perfect for me."[80]

Diamondbacks Achievements

Year-by-Year Records

Regular Season

Season	Wins	Losses	Pct.	Finish	Manager
1998	65	97	.401	5th	Buck Showalter
1999	100	62	.617	1st	Showalter
2000	85	77	.525	3rd	Showalter
2001	92	70	.568	1st	Bob Brenly
2002	98	64	.605	1st	Brenly
2003	84	78	.519	3rd	Brenly

Playoff Records

Year	Division	League	World Series
1999	Lost to NY Mets, 3-1		
2001	Beat St. Louis, 3-2	Beat Atlanta, 4-1	Beat NY Yankees, 4-3
2002	Lost to St. Louis, 3-0		

Team Pitching Records

Strikeouts: Randy Johnson, 1,542
Victories: Randy Johnson, 87
Games: Greg Swindell, 191

Single-Season Offensive Records

Hits: Luis Gonzalez, 206 (1999)
Batting Average: Luis Gonzalez, .336 (1999)
Home Runs: Luis Gonzalez, 57 (2001)
Stolen Bases: Tony Womack, 72 (1999)

Notes

Chapter 1: Winning from the Beginning

1. Quoted in Len Sherman, *Big League, Big Time*. New York: Pocket Books, 1998, p. 95.
2. Quoted in Bob Page, *Tales from the Diamondback Dugout*. Champaign, IL: Sports Publishing, 2002, pp. 15–16.
3. Quoted in "Bouncing Buck: Showalter Fired in Phoenix," Reuters, October 2, 2000. http://abcnewsgo.com.
4. Quoted in Page, *Tales from the Diamondback Dugout*, p. 33.
5. Quoted in Bob Nightengale, "For Diamondbacks, the Time to Strike Is Now," *USA Today Baseball Weekly*, July 18, 2001. www.usatoday.com.
6. Quoted in Nightengale, "For Diamondbacks, the Time to Strike Is Now."
7. Quoted in Page, *Tales from the Diamondback Dugout*, p. 91.
8. Quoted in Bob Nightengale, "Johnson, Schilling Rise to the Occasion," *USA Today Baseball Weekly*, October 23, 2001. www.usatoday.com.
9. Quoted in Page, *Tales from the Diamondback Dugout*, p. 106.
10. Quoted in Seth Livingstone, "Yankees Get a Taste of Their Own Medicine." *USA Today Baseball Weekly*, November 6, 2001. www.usatoday.com.
11. Quoted in Livingstone, "Yankees Get a Taste of Their Own Medicine."
12. Quoted in Seth Livingstone, "2001: A Year Like No Other," *USA Today Baseball Weekly*, December 26, 2001. www.usatoday.com.

Chapter 2: Randy Johnson

13. Quoted in Larry Stone, *Randy Johnson: Arizona Heat!* Champaign, IL: Sports Publishing, 1999, p. 13.
14. Quoted in Matt Christopher, *On the Mound with Randy John-*

son. Boston: Little, Brown, 1998, pp. 20–21.

15. Quoted in Stone, *Randy Johnson: Arizona Heat!*, p. 47.

16. Quoted in Stone, *Randy Johnson: Arizona Heat!*, p. 75.

17. Quoted in Bob Baum, "Alfonso Lifts Mets in Grand Style," Associated Press. www.baseball.ca.

18. Quoted in Tom Verducci, "Raising Arizona," *Sports Illustrated*, November 5, 2001, p. 15.

19. Quoted in Stephen Cannella, "Power Couple," *Sports Illustrated*, November 7, 2001. http://sportsillustrated.cnn.com.

20. Quoted in Wayne Drehs, "Big Unit Learns Valuable Lesson," ESPN.com. http://espn.go.com.

21. Quoted in Seth Livingstone, "The Other Ace Shuts Down Yankee Bats," *USA Today Baseball Weekly*, October 30, 2001. www.usatoday.com.

22. Quoted in Livingstone, "The Other Ace Shuts Down Yankee Bats."

23. Quoted in Livingstone, "The Other Ace Shuts Down Yankee Bats."

24. Quoted in Steve Gilbert, "Big Unit Signs Extension." March 24, 2003. www.mlb.com.

Chapter 3: Curt Schilling

25. Quoted in Page, *Tales from the Diamondback Dugout*, p. 41.

26. Quoted in Paul Hagen, *Curt Schilling: Phillie Phire!* Champaign, IL: Sports Publishing, 1999, p. 17.

27. Quoted in Hagen, *Curt Schilling: Phillie Phire!*, p. 20.

28. Quoted in Nightengale, "For Diamondbacks, the Time to Strike Is Now."

29. Quoted in Nightengale, "For Diamondbacks, the Time to Strike Is Now."

30. Quoted in Nightengale, "For Diamondbacks, the Time to Strike Is Now."

31. Quoted in "Curt Schilling's Letter to America," ESPN.com, September 17, 2001. www.espn.go.com.

32. Quoted in Nightengale, "For Diamondbacks, the Time to Strike Is Now."

33. Quoted in Livingstone, "Yankees Get a Taste of Their Own Medicine."

Chapter 4: Byung-Hyun Kim

34. Quoted in Tim Keown, "Save It!" *ESPN The Magazine.* http://espn.go.com.
35. Quoted in "Kim Byung-hyun Shines in Workout with D-backs," *Korea Times*, March 30, 1999. www.sed.co.kr.
36. Quoted in "Byung-Hyun Kim," Baseballlibrary.com. www.baseballlibrary.com.
37. Quoted in Keown, "Save It!"
38. Quoted in Keown, "Save It!"
39. Quoted in Keown, "Save It!"
40. Quoted in Stephen Cannella, "Saved: Rebounding from Last Fall's Debacle, Byung-Hyun Kim Has a New Weapon: a Hoffmanesque Change," *Sports Illustrated*, May 13, 2002, p. 48.
41. Quoted in Bob Nightengale, "Saving Grace in Arizona." *USA Today Baseball Weekly*, October 10, 2001. www.usatoday.com.
42. Quoted in Seth Livingstone, "Mystique, Aura and Deja Vu Win Another One," *USA Today Baseball Weekly*, November 6, 2001. www.usatoday.com.
43. Quoted in Livingstone, "Mystique, Aura and Deja Vu Win Another One."
44. Quoted in Keown, "Save It!"
45. Quoted in Keown, "Save It!"
46. Quoted in Keown, "Save It!"

Chapter 5: Mark Grace

47. Quoted in Barry Rozner, *Mark Grace: Winning with Grace.* Champaign, IL: Sports Publishing, 1999, pp. 21–22.
48. Quoted in Rozner, *Mark Grace: Winning with Grace*, pp. 26–27.
49. Quoted in Bob Nightengale, "Grace Finds Motivation in Cub's Snub." *USA Today Baseball Weekly*, January 31, 2001. www.usatoday.com.
50. Quoted in Nightengale, "Grace Finds Motivation in Cub's Snub."
51. Quoted in "Baseball Quote of the Day." http://quote.webcircle.com.
52. Quoted in Verducci, "Raising Arizona."

Chapter 6: Matt Williams

53. Quoted in Bob Nightengale, "Arizona Follows Williams to a Championship," *USA Today Baseball Weekly*, November 6, 2001. www.usatoday.com.
54. Quoted in Rob Neyer, "Kent-for-Williams: From Ugly to Beautiful," ESPN.com, September 8, 2002. www.espn.go.com.
55. Quoted in "No Deal: Rockies, D'backs End Talks as Trade Falls Through," SI.com, November 22, 2002. www. sportsillustrated.cnn.com.
56. Quoted in Nightengale, "Arizona Follows Williams to a Championship."
57. Quoted in Bob Nightengale, "How Williams Got His Groove Back," *USA Today Baseball Weekly*, May 5, 1999. www.usatoday.com.
58. Quoted in Nightengale, "Arizona Follows Williams to a Championship."
59. Quoted in Mark Gonzales, "'A Father First,' Williams Retires After 17 Years," *Arizona Republic*, June 13, 2003, p. C-1.
60. Quoted in Gonzales, "'A Father First,' Williams Retires After 17 Years."
61. Quoted in Gonzales, "'A Father First,' Williams Retires After 17 Years."

Chapter 7: Luis Gonzalez

62. Quoted in "When I Was a Kid … An Interview with the Arizona Diamondbacks' Luis Gonzalez." www.juniorbaseball. com.
63. Quoted in Paul White, "Their Paths Diverged, Now Cross Again." *USA Today Baseball Weekly*, October 30, 2001. www.usatoday.com.
64. Quoted in White, "Their Paths Diverged, Now Cross Again."
65. Quoted in White, "Their Paths Diverged, Now Cross Again."
66. Quoted in White, "Their Paths Diverged, Now Cross Again."
67. Quoted in Jeff Bradley, "Cool Breeze." *ESPN The Magazine*. http://espn.go.com/magazine.

68. Quoted in Bradley, "Cool Breeze."
69. Quoted in Bradley, "Cool Breeze."
70. Quoted in Bradley, "Cool Breeze."
71. Quoted in Mike Bauman, "Kids Get Kicks with Gonzo." MLB.com Baseball Perspectives, May 26, 2003. http://mlb.mlb.com.
72. Quoted in Justice B. Hill, "Gonzalez Dethrones Sosa in 2001 Home Run Derby," MLB.com. http://mlb.com.
73. Quoted in Bradley, "Cool Breeze."
74. Quoted in Seth Livingstone, "Popups Make up for Yanks' Lack of Pop," *USA Today Baseball Weekly*, November 6, 2001. www.usatoday.com.
75. Quoted in Page, *Tales from the Diamondback Dugout*, p. 120.
76. Quoted in Page, *Tales from the Diamondback Dugout*, p. 120.
77. Quoted in Jack Macgruder, "Gonzalez, 'Face of D'backs,' Re-signs," *Arizona Daily Star*, March 19, 2003, p. C-1.
78. Quoted in "Left Fielder Agrees to Three-Year, $30M Extension," Associated Press, March 19, 2003. http://espn.go.com.
79. Quoted in John Schlegel, "Give Gonzo Some Credit," MLB.com Baseball Perspectives, July 5, 2003. http://mlb.com.
80. Quoted in Macgruder, "Gonzalez, 'Face of D'backs,' Re-signs."

For Further Reading

Jerry Colangelo with Len Sherman, *How You Play the Game.* New York: AMACOM, 1999. Diamondbacks owner Jerry Colangelo details his rags-to-riches rise to the top. He also describes his particular style of business management.

Bob Crawford, *Arizona Diamondbacks: We're in the Show.* San Francisco: Woodford Press, 1998. The story of the creation of the Diamondbacks, complete with great color photographs.

Mike Lupica, *The Summer of '98.* New York: Putnam, 1999. Touching remembrances of the 1998 Sosa/McGwire home run race and the season that renewed interest in baseball, told through the filter of a father's relationship with his sons.

Tim McCarver and Danny Peary, *The Perfect Season.* New York: Villard, 1999. Sportscaster and former catcher McCarver describes why 1998 was perhaps the greatest season in baseball history.

John Nichols, *The History of the Arizona Diamondbacks.* Mankato, MN: Creative Education, 2000. A very short history of the first years of the Diamondbacks organization.

Larry Stone, *Randy Johnson: Arizona Heat!* Sports Publishing, 1999. A youth-oriented biography of Randy Johnson.

Works Consulted

Books

Matt Christopher, *On the Mound with Randy Johnson*. Boston: Little, Brown, 1998. Good biography covering Johnson's pre-Diamondbacks baseball career.

Paul Hagen, *Curt Schilling: Phillie Phire!* Champaign, IL: Sports Publishing, 1999. Good, short biography covering Schilling's early baseball career.

David S. Neft, Richard M. Cohen, and Michael L. Neft, *The Sports Encyclopedia: Baseball 2003*. New York: St. Martin's Griffin, 2003. Volume that contains season records, team records, World Series game records, and almost any statistic a baseball fan might need.

Bob Page, *Tales from the Diamondback Dugout*. Champaign, IL: Sports Publishing, 2002. Page tells many insider stories that have never been recounted in print. Good resource of previously unknown materials.

Barry Rozner, *Mark Grace: Winning with Grace*. Champaign, IL: Sports Publishing, 1999. Good, short biography covering Grace's pre-Diamondbacks baseball career.

Len Sherman, *Big League, Big Time*. New York: Pocket Books, 1998. Invaluable resource for behind-the-scenes information on the creation of the Diamondbacks. Sherman has a wry humor and a keen appreciation for the absurd.

Internet Sources

"Byung-Hyun Kim," Baseballlibrary.com, www.baseball library.com.

"Curt Schilling," Baseballlibrary.com, www.baseballlibrary.com.

"Curt Schilling's Letter to America," ESPN.com, September 17, 2001, www.espn.go.com.

Steve Gilbert, "Big Unit Signs Extension," MLB.com, March 24, 2004, www.baseballstation.com.

"Kim Byung-hyun Shines in Workout With D-backs," *Korea Times*, March 30, 1999, www.sed.co.kr.

"Mark Grace," Baseballlibrary.com, www.baseballlibrary.com.

"Matt Williams," Baseballlibrary.com, www.baseballlibrary.com.

Rob Neyer, "Kent-for-Williams: From Ugly to Beautiful," ESPN.com, September 8, 2002, www.espn.go.com.

Bob Nightengale, "How Williams Got His Groove Back," *USA Today Baseball Weekly*, May 5, 1999, www.usatoday.com.

———, "Grace Finds Motivation in Cubs' Snub," *USA Today Baseball Weekly*, January 31, 2001, www.usatoday.com.

———, "Arizona Follows Williams to a Championship," *USA Today Baseball Weekly*, November 6, 2001, www. usatoday.com.

"Randy Johnson," Baseballlibrary.com, www.baseballlibrary.com.

"Rockies, D'backs End Talks as Trade Falls Through," SI.com, November 22, 2002, www.sportsillustrated.cnn.com.

Website

Major League Baseball (www.mlb.com). The official site of Major League Baseball is a good source for player and team news, statistics, and analysis.

Index

Picture Credits

About the Author

Christopher Higgins lives and writes in Haddonfield, New Jersey. He is a stay-at-home dad to daughter Talia, a freelance writer and editor, a graduate student, an elementary school teacher, and a baseball fanatic. When not writing, he can often be found in one of Philadelphia's great used bookstores or Indian restaurants.